THE SWORD AND THE PL

Autonomous Peace Initiatives in East Germany

THE SWORD AND THE PLOUGHSHARE
AUTONOMOUS PEACE INITIATIVES IN EAST GERMANY

John Sandford

United States distributor
DUFOUR EDITIONS, INC.
Booksellers and Publishers
Chester Springs, PA 19425
215-458-5005

MERLIN PRESS/EUROPEAN NUCLEAR DISARMAMENT
LONDON

British Library Cataloguing in Publication Data

Sandford, John
    The sword and the ploughshare
    1. Peace—Societies, etc.—20th century
    2. Germany, East—Politics and government
    I. Title
    327.1'72'09431087   JX1908.E/

Published jointly by
END/Merlin Press
3 Manchester Road
London   E14

Cover design by Louis Mackay

Typesetting by Heather Hems
The Malt House
Chilmark
Wilts

Printed by Whitstable Litho
Whitstable
Kent

ISBN 0-85036-303-9

CONTENTS

THE SWORD AND THE PLOUGHSHARE

Autonomous Peace Initiatives in East Germany

BACKGROUND

The Country

The territory of the present-day German Democratic Republic corresponds to the Zone of Germany occupied from 1945 to 1949—in accordance with the Yalta Agreement of February 1945—by the Soviet Union, plus the formerly Soviet-occupied Eastern Sector of Berlin, which today forms the country's capital. In area (41,576 square miles) the Soviet Zone was somewhat under half the size of the Western Zones—occupied by Britain, the US, and France—which were later to become the Federal Republic of Germany. The present population of the GDR—some 17 million—compares with 61 million in the Federal Republic.

One of the main aims agreed on by the wartime Allies was the eradication for once and for all of fascism and militarism, and the 'democratisation' of Germany: for the Soviet Union these objectives could only be ensured by the creation of a Socialist system, and accordingly, as power was handed back to the Germans, Socialists, and especially Communists, were increasingly favoured. Thoroughgoing reforms of industry, agriculture, education, and the legal system accompanied and assisted this process. As another of the Allies' declared aims had been the eventual re-establishment of a united Germany, the Soviet Union and the East German Communists were anxious to create a *fait accompli* in the form of a Socialist system that could be adopted by—or at least shape—the whole country.

The beginnings of the Cold War and the division of Europe and the world into two increasingly antagonistic blocs meant the abandonment for the time being of hopes for a reunited Germany under Communist control. In May 1949 the Federal Republic was founded in the West; just over four months later, on 7 October 1949, the German Democratic Republic was founded in the East.

The domestic history of the GDR since then has seen the consolidation of Communist control and the coordination of virtually all areas of life in accordance with Marxist-Leninist principles. This has not however been a simple linear process, and it is possible to discern overall a series of pendulum swings between tightening and relaxation of the system. The 1950s, the decade in which the Party was consolidating its hold on the country, were a relatively 'tight' period. This was the decade that witnessed the one major public manifestation of popular discontent in the GDR's history: the events of 17 June 1953. Classified in the West as an 'uprising', and in the East as an attempted 'counter-revolutionary coup', the disturbances were quelled with the assistance of Soviet troops. A less spectacular but in the long term more damaging manifestation of popular discontent was the refugee problem: by the beginning of the sixties some three million people had left the GDR—in particular across the still-open border in the divided city of Berlin. Many of them were young, educated, and skilled. As middle-class professionals, they knew they could sell themselves more profitably in the Federal Republic, and many resented the positive discrimination that had been applied in favour of the previously under-privileged working classes in the GDR in such areas as education. Their loss was doing immense damage to the East German economy. In August 1961 the border was finally sealed with the erection of a heavily-guarded wall across Berlin.

Many in the West assumed that the erection of the wall would lead to sullen resentment and possible rebellion in the East. In the event August 1961 turned out to be a major turning-point not only in the history of the GDR, but in East–West relations in general. Resentment there undoubtedly was, but more important was a new determination among East Germans to 'make a go of it' in their own country now that emigration to the West was no longer an open option. The economy picked up, giving the GDR the highest standard of living in Eastern Europe, and Western visitors began noticing a growing willingness on the part of East Germans to identify with 'their' GDR, to take pride in its achievements, and to defend it indignantly against the arrogant West German paternalism that still insisted it was merely the 'Soviet Zone of Occupation'. On the international level the Berlin Wall helped—albeit in a singularly brutal fashion—to solve one of the great outstanding problems of the Cold War years. Today the erection of the 'Anti-Fascist Protective Wall' is celebrated in the GDR as a major contribution to the East–West 'détente' of the 1960s.

The 1960s were accordingly an era of—on the whole— greater liberalisation in the domestic life of the GDR. Externally there still remained the problem of recognition: the GDR enjoyed diplomatic relations with few states outside the Communist world, not least because of the West German 'Hallstein Doctrine', which refused relations with any country that recognised the GDR. The coming in 1969 of the first Social Democrat-led government in West Germany led quickly to an easing of relations between the two German states, and in the early seventies, largely through the 'Ostpolitik' initiatives of Willy Brandt, the West Germans finally abandoned the pretence that the GDR did not exist.

Until the 1970s the leading figure in East German politics had been the veteran Communist Walter Ulbricht. In 1971 the ageing Ulbricht (who died in 1973) was replaced as First Secretary of the Party by Erich Honecker; in 1976 Honecker was also elected Chairman of the Council of State. This position—*de facto* that of Head of State—coupled with his position as top man in the Party, means that Erich Honecker has the supreme authority in both the ruling hierarchies— State and Party—in the GDR system.

The 1970s saw a steady increase in the material prosperity of the East German people; they did not, however, see the increase in the liberalisation of political life that had seemed apparent at the start of the decade. One of the main reasons for this was, oddly enough, the 'normalisation' of relations with the West. It became quickly apparent to the authorities that the opening to the West could be misinterpreted as a step towards German reunification via a 'convergence' of the systems. The 'normalisation' of inter-German relations was thus accompanied in the East by a firm official insistence that the GDR and the Federal Republic were two quite separate states, of which the GDR, as a Socialist state, was historically the more advanced, with its own distinctive culture, and its own historical roots in the progressive forces of German history. Even the Constitution had to be rewritten, dropping the description of the GDR as 'a Socialist state of the German nation', and substituting 'a Socialist state of the workers and farmers'.

Internally, there ensued an increasingly thorough imposition of ideological norms on all areas of public life. This was a process that was felt particularly by the country's intellectual community, and when, in November 1976, the critical poet and singer Wolf Biermann was deprived of his GDR citizenship whilst on a concert tour of West Germany, there was a quite unprecedented outcry. Several of the country's leading writers protested openly at the expulsion of Biermann, and, by the end of the decade, a good number of them had—with what amounted virtually to positive encouragement on the part of the Government—left the GDR to take up residence in the Federal Republic. Those who stayed behind were by no means all unquestioning adherents of the Party line: awkward, critical voices, some of whom have become important figures in the peace movement, still remain. Their works often remain unpublished in the East, but are readily available in the West—again with the ready consent of the GDR authorities, who see advantages in this arrangement both for their image and their bank balance.

In the 1970s it became increasingly apparent that what distinguished the GDR more than anything else from the other countries of Eastern Europe was the peculiar links it had with the West. The process of 'Abgrenzung'—of drawing a clear ideological line between the two German states—had been felt imperative by the East German authorities in view of the increasing contacts that their citizens were now having with West Germany and West Germans. Under the various agreements that resulted from the 'Ostpolitik' initiatives it was made considerably easier for West Germans and West Berliners to visit the GDR. Many West Germans have friends and relations in the GDR, and in the 1970s they began coming to visit them in large numbers—and often forming further friendships as a result. Thus by the end of the seventies some three and a half million visits to the GDR were being made each year by West Germans, and a similar number by West Berliners. For East Germans to visit the West is more difficult, but provisions do exist for individuals to do so 'on urgent family business'—which includes births, deaths, serious illness, marriage, and important wedding anniversaries of near relatives. These arrangements have meant that on average somewhat over 40,000 people a year have been able to make visits to the West since the mid-seventies. For pensioners there are no requirements to be fulfilled and trips to the West by them have averaged around one and a third million per year over the same period.

These facts and figures are important, and it is vital to appreciate that this relative openness to the West is one of the most distinctive facts about the GDR. It is something that makes it a very different country from its neighbours and allies in Eastern Europe, for not only is there a very high degree of contact with Westerners, but it is moreover contact that can take place within the privacy of the home, that can be conducted in a common language, and that often enjoys the privileged intimacy of the family reunion. But there is another, and in some ways even more important, openness to the West that makes the East Germans a very different people from other East Europeans, and that is the phenomenon that has been described in the West as 'the nightly reunion of the German people around the television set'. The mass media of the GDR are very much instruments of ideological control: both broadcasting and the press are allotted the threefold task—based on a dictum of Lenin's—of 'propaganda, agitation, and organisation'. Western newspapers and magazines are to all intents and purposes unobtainable: they cannot be bought or subscribed to, and Westerners trying to take them across the border are liable to have them confiscated. Yet this hermetic system is quite unable to keep out Western radio and television signals. Radio has of course always played a role in the propaganda war between East and West, but geographical proximity and the fact of the common language mean that East Germans are not restricted to propaganda services such as that of the American-controlled German station 'RIAS' in West

5

Berlin: they can also 'drop in' on West German domestic services.

But more significantly, the East Germans can also 'drop in' on the three West German television services. And 'drop in' they do: although official figures are not available, it is widely assumed that East Germans regularly watch West German television as much as, if not more than, their own two channels. Signals from West German television reach most of the GDR, either from the powerful transmitters that the West Germans have built obligingly close to the border, or from the transmitters in West Berlin. Only one significant area of the GDR is beyond the range of West German television, and that is the south-eastern corner of the country. Indeed, rumour has it that Dresden, which lies in this area, is for this reason a city that many people hope they will not have to move to.

Contrary to a widespread misapprehension in the West, watching Western television is not illegal in the GDR. Indeed, it is such a basic fact of life that the authorities have long come to terms with it. This is evidenced for instance by the broadcasting on East German television of a programme called 'The Black Channel', which shows and then analyses extracts from West German television in an attempt to ensure at least that East Germans will not view Western programmes entirely uncritically. Further evidence that Western television is accepted as there to stay is provided by the availability of colour sets that are adjustable to both the 'PAL' and 'SECAM' standards, the only conceivable advantage of which is that they will pick up Western programmes—on the 'PAL' standard—in colour, something that standard East German 'SECAM' sets cannot do. Similarly, there are now signs that the practice of rigging communal aerials on blocks of flats to pick up GDR programmes only— and leaving it to individual households to erect their own aerials indoors or on their balconies for the Western programmes—is being abandoned in favour of providing *all* available services over the communal aerial. Preliminary plans for the cabling of East German cities even indicate that the cable networks too will carry Western television.

Of course, some other East Europeans can also watch

Western television: in certain areas of Czechoslovakia it is possible to watch West German and Austrian television; parts of Hungary are also reached by Austrian transmissions. But there is a world of difference between small groups of Czechs and Hungarians being able to pick up programmes in a foreign language, and the ready availability to the great majority of the East German population of three complete Western services *in their own language.* This is a state of affairs quite without parallel in Eastern Europe, and leads East Germans to claim—with some justification—that they are the best-informed people in the world, being able to survey the Eastern viewpoint in their morning papers, and compare it with the Western offerings on television in the evening.

Undoubtedly this implies a somewhat idealised view of the workings of television, and there is evidence of an uncritical assumption amongst some East Germans that television's glossy images of daily life are an accurate reflection of the way things are in the West. More to the point though is the importance of the *information* that West German television can bring the East Germans. Sometimes this duplicates the information already available in their own media, as for instance in the reports on the Western peace movements that have had such an effect on the peace movement in the GDR itself (though only the anti-NATO demands get reported in the GDR). But much more significant is the information that Western television often carries about events in the GDR itself—things that the East German media pass over in silence, deeming them not conducive to the cause of Socialism. West German television has thus been of particular importance for the autonomous peace movement in the GDR: its gatherings and statements quickly become common knowledge when reported on West German television. Indeed, so assiduous is West German television at registering the slightest tremor of dissent in the GDR that small peace gatherings can be assured of a degree of publicity beyond the wildest dreams of Western peace activists. Critical voices in the East have quite consciously used the Western media as the only channel open to them to reach their own fellow-citizens. Typical of this approach is a plea made by Robert

7

Havemann for help in publicising the 'Berlin Appeal'—a plea that is also typical in its sanguine assumptions about the influence that Westerners have on 'their' broadcasting services:

> We address ourselves to our friends in the peace movement in the West, to writers, scientists, representatives of the Christian Churches, indeed to everyone who has appreciated that forces for peace throughout the world will receive a powerful impetus from a free peace movement in the GDR. . . . Use every means at your disposal to provide the people of the GDR—via West German radio and tv—with the important facts about our peace movement. Disseminate this article in radio broadcasts, and arrange interviews on television about the Berlin Appeal with writers, scientists, politicians, and theologians.'
>
> (Quoted in Büscher et al., 228f.)

The State

For all its openness to the West—or perhaps *because* of it— East Germany's official ideology is a sombrely orthodox brand of Marxism-Leninism. The relations between State and citizen, and the guiding principles behind the overall organisation of public life are summed up clearly in the opening words of the country's Constitution:

> The German Democratic Republic is a Socialist state of workers and farmers. It is the political organization of the working people in town and country under the leadership of the working class and its Marxist-Leninist Party.

Two points are of particular relevance here. The first is the designation of the GDR as a *'Socialist* state'. 'Socialism' has a very wide range of meanings in the West; in East German parlance, as here in the Constitution, it means something quite specific—the stage in historical development that lies between the capitalist past and the Communist future. In 'Socialist' society the groundwork is laid for Communism; the fundamental contradictions of capitalist society are overcome, but because some problems still remain, and because

8

of the constant threat from the still-existing capitalist countries elsewhere in the world, the Socialist state has to be strong and disciplined. And this is where the second point comes in: the 'leadership of the working class and its Marxist-Leninist Party'. The logic behind this assignation of ultimate power to the Party runs something like this: history is not an arbitrary succession of random contingencies; instead it follows laws of development that enable us not only to account for the past, but also to anticipate the future; these laws were analysed supremely by Marx and Engels, who noted that with the rise of the working class there was for the first time in the history of class society a class whose interests coincided with those of all humankind; once it came to political power, the working class could therefore institute a society in which the antagonisms, exploitation, and class divisions of previous stages of history would be eliminated; the working class exercises its political power through its Party; the tactics and strategy of the Party were analysed and practised supremely by Lenin; given these facts, and given that history is moving towards Communism anyway, it is perverse to refuse to get in step with the tide of events—rather it is imperative to accept the leadership of the Party, which is made up of people who have grasped these insights more clearly than others, and who are therefore acting in accordance with the dictates of history and the well-being of humanity.

The implications behind the important first article of the GDR's Constitution are vital for an understanding of the official attitude to—and handling of—socio-political initiatives within the country that do not originate from the Party: initiatives such as the autonomous peace movement. Ideas and activities that can be construed as incompatible with the ideals of the 'Socialist state' or the 'leadership of the . . . Marxist-Leninist Party' find themselves sailing very close to the winds not only of legality but of constitutionality too in the GDR. And since the Party is assigned the leading role in the state, the Party is the ultimate arbiter of what *is* 'Socialist', and thus also of what is anti-Socialist—and therefore anti-constitutional.

It is in this context that one has to view the civil rights

guaranteed to citizens of the GDR by the country's Constitution. Those that an autonomous peace movement might want to take its stand on—freedom of expression, freedom of assembly, freedom of association—are all there. Thus Article 27, on freedom of opinion, states:

> Every citizen of the German Democratic Republic has the right, in accordance with the principles of this Constitution, to express his opinion freely and in public.

The vital element in this proclamation is the qualification 'in accordance with the principles of this Constitution'. What those principles are has already been made clear in Article 1. Similarly Article 28, on freedom of assembly:

> All citizens have the right to peaceful assembly, within the bounds of the principles and aims of the Constitution.

And as for freedom of association, that too is bounded by the obligation to accord with the 'principles and aims of the Constitution' in Article 29:

> The citizens of the German Democratic Republic have the right of association, in order to realise their interests through common action in political parties, social organisations, associations and collectives, in accordance with the principles and aims of the Constitution.

In fact it is virtually impossible to found a new organisation in the GDR: it would either fall foul of the 'principles and aims of the Constitution' provision, or it would be deemed unnecessary, as all aspects of social and political life are considered to be catered for by the existing organisations— which are ultimately accountable to the Party. Such organisations include the 'mass organisations' like the Free German Youth (FDJ) and the Free German Trade Union Federation (FDGB)—which between them cover the great bulk of the population—and the political parties. It is often assumed in the West that all Communist countries are—like the Soviet Union—one-party states. In a sense this is true, in that all accord ultimate authority to *the* Party, but some nonetheless at the same time operate a 'Socialist multi-party system'. The GDR is an example of this: in addition to the SED— the Marxist-Leninist 'Socialist Unity Party of Germany', which came into being in 1946 as a Soviet-backed fusion of the Communist and Social Democrat parties—there are four other political parties in the country. The reasons for this are partly historical and partly tactical: the GDR is not only a country that had a strong middle class, but it also—unlike for instance the Soviet Union — had, within living memory, a multi-party parliamentary system; accordingly, during the period of Soviet occupation political parties were established to provide a 'home' for those segments of the population who might find it difficult to accommodate to the idea of living in a state that professed itself to be run by and for the working class. The four parties thus cater between them for the middle classes, for the Christian community, for the rural population, and for those of a nationalist disposition. Their membership hovers around the 100,000 mark; that of the SED is around 2 million.

The GDR does not claim to be a classless society: that is something that will come about with 'Communism', but is not yet a feature of 'Socialism'. However, classes—and other social groups—within 'Socialism' are no longer antagonistic as they were under capitalism. For this reason the 'Socialist multi-party system' is not comparable with the multi-party systems of the West. The parties in the GDR do not compete with one another, and they certainly do not compete with the SED: they all accept its leadership and its role as the guiding force in the land. Their function is rather to win over to the cause of Socialism those groupings within the population whose instinctive allegiances may lie elsewhere: to make themselves redundant, in fact.

It is not possible to vote for the party of one's choice in elections as happens in the West: as the parties cooperate rather than compete, that would not make sense. Instead, voters are presented with a common electoral programme drawn up jointly by the political parties and the mass organisations; the proposals are open to amendment during the period of intense, but carefully organised, public debate

11

that takes place during the run-up to the elections. The actual casting of one's vote thus gives final legitimacy to decisions that have in effect already been taken: it is rather like 'agreeing the minutes' of a meeting that has already taken place. The pressure to go and vote is enormous: the turnout is normally around 99 per cent. The pressure to vote 'Yes' is equally overwhelming: around 99 per cent of voters normally do so. And since they are not voting for individual parties, the way they vote does not affect the number of seats each party and mass organisation has in the People's Chamber: the allocation of seats is predetermined in order to give a 'fair' representation to the various groupings within the population. And since, again, the parties do not compete, it does not matter that the SED is actually outnumbered by three to one by the other groupings in the Chamber: voting is always unanimous.

Or nearly always. Although it is incumbent upon members of the People's Chamber to make their decisions in accordance with 'the objective laws of social development', there is one recorded instance of a non-unanimous vote. This was in 1972, when 14 out of the 500 members voted against a proposal to liberalise the abortion laws, and a further eight abstained. It was a unique occasion, when members of the Christian Democratic Union (CDU) found their Christian principles at odds with those of the SED. That the issue at stake was an ethical rather than a directly political matter saved the day. The fourteen dissenting votes did not need to be classified as 'opposition'. If they had been, then something would have been seriously wrong, for, according to a standard East German political textbook:

In Socialist states there is no objective political or social basis for opposition, for the working class—in alliance with all other working people—is the class in control and at the same time the principle productive force in society.

(*Kleines Politisches Wörterbuch,* 652)

The Church

In a country where there is deemed to be no basis for opposition, no need—and therefore no possibility—to set up new political groupings, and where the exercise of the civil rights of free speech, assembly and association is constitutionally subordinate to the self-defined interests of a single ruling party, there would seem to be precious little room for independent peace initiatives of the type now familiar in the West, especially if they are in any way critical of their own state. What such movements need is, both literally and metaphorically, a 'space' within which to function. In the GDR they have found that space in the Protestant churches.

Since 1964 the official census has stopped recording the number of Christians in the GDR. In that year, out of a total population of about 17 million, just over 11 million were returned as belonging to one of the Christian Churches. Today, with the total population more or less unchanged, it is estimated that there are around 8 million Christians in the GDR—though the criterion for defining a 'Christian' is the somewhat generous one of unrevoked baptism. The GDR belongs to the traditionally Protestant part of Germany, and just under 7 million out of this total are members of what in Germany is referred to as the 'Evangelical' Church: about one in ten of these are active churchgoers; roughly another 100,000 are members of the 'Free' Churches, of which the two largest are the Methodists and the Baptists. The remaining one million or so Christians are accounted for by the Catholic Church.

Marxism-Leninism, the state philosophy of the GDR, is atheist. Religion is seen as a manifestation of the alienation inherent in earlier stages of society, where—as the much-cited 'opium of the people'—it serves to stifle revolutionary fervour and insight with its promises of rewards in the afterlife that are directly proportional to the degradation suffered here on earth. Yet the official figures of 1964, and the unofficial subsequent ones, suggest that religion still plays a not insignificant role in the Socialist GDR. The official explanation for this is that old ways of thinking die hard: the preconditions for religious belief may have been abolished,

13

but it may be some time before the belief itself has died out:

> Even in Socialist society religion still continues to function. The inertia of tradition, external influences, and certain variations in the development of awareness are the reason for this. The dying-out of religion can only be a lengthy process. The decisive role in this is played by the practical re-shaping of all the circumstances in which we live by conscious acts of the working people.
>
> (*Kleines Politisches Wörterbuch*, 761)

There has been no real attempt to 'abolish' religion by administrative means in the GDR. The existence of the Churches is accepted, and, as far as possible, turned to best advantage by the State. The underlying assumption that they are transient remnants of an earlier society is, if anything, played down in official public pronouncements; instead, a positive role is found for religion in Socialist society. Emphasis is placed on the progressive elements in the Christian tradition, and parallels are drawn between the socio-ethical teachings of the Church and the humanist principles of Marxism.

This does not mean that relations between Church and State have been easy in the GDR. Nor does it mean that practising one's religion there is an easy matter. Discrimination against Christians in education and careers is widespread, and pressure is frequently brought to bear on parents who send their children to Sunday School—and not infrequently on the children themselves. But it still remains true that the Churches in the GDR enjoy more freedom and more privileges than anywhere else in Eastern Europe, with the possible exception of Poland.

The history of Church/State relations in the GDR is primarily the history of relations between the State and the *Protestant* Churches, not merely because of their numerical superiority, but also because the Catholic Church has tended to keep its head down and avoid areas of contention by confining its activities to the narrowly religious sphere. Not that this attitude has escaped criticism: this has been especially vocal in the 'Halle Action Circle' (*Aktions-*

14

kreis Halle), a Catholic 'ginger group' founded in the late sixties by a small number of clerics and lay people, which, in May 1982, issued a statement calling for a more open involvement by the Church in the current peace debate. (For important recent developments in the Catholic Church see Postscript.) So far, Christian participation in this debate has been left almost exclusively to the Evangelical Church—or rather the Evangelical *Churches,* for the Federation of Evangelical Churches (Bund der Evangelischen Kirchen in der DDR) is made up of eight independent regions. In keeping with a longstanding Lutheran tradition, the Evangelical Church has been at pains to exert its influence on affairs of state where these have involved issues of major relevance to the Christian conscience. Initially it encountered major difficulties: in the 1950s in particular the newly-founded State sought to stress the atheistic implications of its philosophy, and accordingly subjected the Church to considerable repression. The situation was slightly easier in the sixties, but the State was particularly suspicious of the Church's all-German links—a suspicion that was not allayed until 1969 when the West German and East German Evangelical Churches finally went their separate ways, and the present-day East German Bund der Evangelischen Kirchen was established.

Now that the Church is an *East* German Church (though loose links with West Germany are still maintained), it has been possible for it to define more clearly its status within the country, and its attitude to the State and the official ideology. The most concise statement of the Church's position was made in 1971 by the then Bishop of Berlin, Albrecht Schönherr, who proclaimed: 'We do not wish to be a Church alongside Socialism, nor a Church against Socialism: we wish to be a Church within Socialism.' Schönherr's phrase— *Kirche im Sozialismus*—has been repeated and analysed many times since, and remains to this day the cornerstone of the Church's attitudes to the State, and of its relations to the society around it. It makes clear that the Church recognises the Socialist system as a *fait accompli* in the GDR, but that this recognition does not mean, on the one hand, a withdrawal into indifference, nor, on the other hand, does it

15

imply opposition to the system. Instead, the Church will play its role within, and on the basis of, the facts as it finds them; and this it will do—to quote another much-used phrase—in a spirit of 'critical solidarity', or 'critical participation'.

On 6 March 1978, the executive of the Bund der Evangelischen Kirchen had a lengthy meeting with Erich Honecker and other leading representatives of the State and the Party. The internal political atmosphere in the GDR at the time was not good: the aftermath of the expulsion of Wolf Biermann was still very much in the air, and the Christian community was still stunned by the news that a pastor by the name of Oskar Brüsewitz had set fire to himself outside a church in Zeitz in August 1976: his tragic death was an untypically spectacular manifestation of despair at the petty and not so petty acts of discrimination to which members of the Church had repeatedly been subjected. Honecker's invitation was obviously designed to clear the air: it was the first time such a high-level meeting between Church and State had taken place, and it laid the groundwork for future relations between the two. In what was clearly a response to the Church's formula of the 'Church within Socialism', Honecker spoke of the Church as 'a self-supporting organisation of social significance in Socialist society'. The words were—as always—carefully chosen. 'Self-supporting' is here a translation of the German 'eigenständig', which has implications of 'standing on its own two feet'; the word 'indepentent'—'unabhängig'—is studiously avoided, as that would imply that there is nothing *above* the Church. This subtle but crucial distinction has—as we shall see—been brought to bear recently in official designations of the status of the peace movement in the GDR. Also significant is Honecker's description of the Church's status as 'social': the implication here is that the Church's sphere of action does not—and cannot—extend to the realm of *politics*.

The legal position of the Church in the GDR is defined as follows in the country's Constitution:

Every citizen of the German Democratic Republic has the right to profess a religious belief and to perform acts of religion.

16

The Churches and other religious bodies shall organise their own affairs and carry out their activities in accordance with the Constitution and laws of the GDR.

(Article 39)

The 'in accordance with the Constitution' is familiar enough; the meeting with Erich Honecker went some way towards clarifying how, given that provision, the Churches can 'organise their own affairs'. A number of outstanding issues were resolved, and the significant concession was made that the Church would in future be given air time once a month on the state radio and television service to broadcast its own information bulletins—this in addition to the weekly religious service already broadcast on radio, something quite unique in Eastern Europe.

The meeting of 6 March 1978 confirmed that the Church in the GDR enjoys a status that has no parallel elsewhere in the country. It alone is an organisation that is not under the direct control of the Party; it alone is allowed to run its own affairs, to own meeting places and land; to make statements, to produce—for its internal use—leaflets and notices, and to organise events in a manner that does not necessarily conform with the official philosophy of Marxism-Leninism. The Church, in other words, is the sole officially recognised 'space' for the articulation of 'unofficial' ideas.

2

THE PEACE MOVEMENT

The Official View

It is a central tenet of Marxist-Leninist thought that wars result from the antagonisms and contradictions that have been finally overcome in Socialist societies. This was one of the ostensible reasons for the Soviet Union's establishment of a Socialist system in their zone of occupation after the Second World War: the Allies had agreed to destroy once and for all Germany's potential to wage war; since the root causes of war now lay in the capitalist system, the eradication of capitalism was the surest way to eradicate war itself. The GDR thus prides itself on being a 'peace state'; its very existence is seen as a guarantee that—in the words of a familiar slogan, derived from the Potsdam Agreement—'never again shall a war emanate from German soil'. Or at least not from *East* German soil, for the capitalist, and therefore potentially war-mongering, *West* German state means that that threat has still not been totally banished. In Socialist states, no one can profit from the arms race, and the GDR in any case has no armaments industry.

Another slogan—long familiar to visitors to the GDR—proclaims: 'The stronger Socialism is, the more secure is Peace!' This follows logically enough from the above-mentioned assumptions about the indissolubility of Socialism and peace. And to take the argument a step further, it also follows that anything that can be construed as an attack on Socialism is at the same time a threat to peace. And since 'Socialism' is equated with, and defined by, the Marxist-Leninist State, it further follows that the 'strength' being talked about here is ultimately the military might of the GDR and its allies, and that threats to peace can therefore be discerned not only in anything that might weaken the country's ability to wage war in defence of Socialism, but also in any questioning of its political system.

Clearly such a state of affairs poses some important problems for any would-be independent peace movement, for the moment it criticises government policy and makes proposals for disarmament—as independent peace movements are wont to do—it is automatically wrong-footed and decried as a threat to peace, or worse. Such reactions from governments are not unfamiliar in the West as well: here too the authorities in their wisdom are prone to dismiss the peace movements as 'well-intentioned but misguided'—or worse— and thus *in fact* more likely to bring about war than peace. The difference lies in the fact that in the East the authorities can back up their contentions with an awesome ideological construct that also happens to be the official philosophy of the State.

The notion that peace and socialism are not only indivisible, but also preconditions of one another, is absolutely central to the GDR's foreign policy and to the official view of the peace movement:

> The history of the peace movement in the past one hundred years has shown that the struggle for peace, if it is separated from the social struggle of the working class, will be politically ineffectual.
>
> . . . Even today, after a mighty bulwark of peace has developed in the shape of the Soviet Union, the Socialist community and all other forces for peace, the threat to peace emanates from imperialism, which attempts with all the means at its disposal, by a policy of 'rolling back' Socialism and the repression of national liberation movements, to hold up the inevitable development of human society towards Socialism and Communism.
>
> . . . The further strengthening of the Socialist world system provides the real possibility—by means of the common struggle of all peace-loving people—of banishing world war from the life of society.
>
> *(Kleines Politisches Wörterbuch,* 254f.)

In order to promote these ideas both nationally and internationally, there exists in the GDR a body called the 'Peace Council of the GDR' (Friedensrat der DDR). Similar bodies exist in all other East European countries, and all are affiliated to the Helsinki-based 'World Peace Council'. Affiliates

19

of the WPC are in fact to be found in most countries of the world, where their critics tend to dismiss them as 'Moscow-front organisations'. The Peace Council of the GDR, which is organisationally linked with the Soviet Peace Council, is certainly—like other WPC affiliates—wedded to the philosophy that Socialism equals Peace, and thus to support for the foreign policy of the Soviet Union and its allies. It is officially described as 'the embodiment of the desire for peace of the people of the GDR in accordance with the peace policies of the Socialist State' (*Kleines Politisches Wörter-buch,* 257). In a recent English-language brochure, widely distributed in the West, if affirms its identity with the policies of the State in the following terms:

> In the socialist German Democratic Republic the peaceful policies of the state and the people's desire for peace are two sides of the same coin. Peace and socialism go together. Under socialist conditions the policies of the state are identical with the objectives of the peace movement.

This state of affairs, it goes on to proclaim,

> is hardly to the liking of the opponents of détente and the advocates of NATO's arms build-up. Hence their call for the establishment of an 'independent peace movement' in an apparent attempt to disrupt the joint striving for peace by the government and the people and to set up some kind of political opposition donning the mantle of peacemaker.
>
> (*Who is threatening whom?,* Published by the Peace Council of the German Democratic Republic, Berlin 1982, 40f.)

Not surprisingly, the Peace Council is frequently described in the West as the 'official' peace movement in the GDR, with the implication that peace initiatives such as those associated with the 'Swords into Ploughshares' badge are the 'unofficial' peace movement. The Peace Council's own state-ments certainly point to this conclusion, but at the same time it·would be a mistake to try to draw too sharp a line between the two. Indeed, recent events in the GDR have shown that both sides, for different reasons, have been doing their best to *avoid* an overt polarisation. Western affiliates of the World Peace Council tend to be single-mindedly orthodox in their attitudes. It would be wrong to deduce that the same necessarily holds true of Eastern affiliates such as the GDR Peace Council: operating as it does within a system that provides no other outlets for the organised expression of peace movement attitudes, it contains within its ranks a greater pluralism of opinion than may be apparent from its external image.

What does distinguish the Peace Council from autonomous initiatives is the fact that it, unlike them, is able to take full advantage of the provisions of Article 28 of the Constitution —the Article on freedom of assembly—that guarantee 'the use of the material preconditions for the free exercise of this right: places of assembly, streets, squares, printing presses and news media'. These privileges it enjoys because it alone is deemed to be operating unambiguously 'in accordance with the principles and aims of the Constitution' by presenting a public face that accords implicitly with government policy. Although the Peace Council is not itself classified as a 'mass organisation', it is made up of representatives of all the important groupings in society, and is thus able to mobilise large segments of the population at very short notice. This it did, to take two typical examples, in the autumn of 1979 when a petition in support of Soviet disarmament proposals was presented to—and signed by—practically every adult in the GDR (ninety-six per cent of those over fourteen had signed within a month), and again at Whitsun 1982 when throughout the country hundreds of thousands of children and young people took part in organised demonstrations against NATO policy. Both of these operations were distinguished by the fact that they were:

(1) organised on a massive, country-wide scale;
(2) coordinated from above;
(3) directed solely against the military policies of the West;
(4) wholly affirmative towards the military policies of the East.

If there *are* features that are diagnostic of an 'official' peace movement in the GDR, then it is points such as these; and if one is to look for an autonomous, or 'unofficial', peace movement, then the absence of these characteristics is a good starting point.

The Autonomous Peace Movement

The Western media, and particularly the West German media, first began talking of an 'autonomous', 'unofficial', or 'independent' peace movement in the GDR in the early part of 1982. Two incidents in particular had attracted their attention: the first was the launching in East Berlin of the 'Berlin Appeal'; the second, following soon after, was a 'Peace Forum' which attracted some 5,000 young people to a church in Dresden. Comparisons were drawn with what was happening in the West—in particular with the circulation in West Germany of the 'Krefeld Appeal', and the massive gatherings of young people at peace demonstrations there. Evidence of spontaneous initiatives in the East was most welcome to the Western peace movements, but both the over-hasty comparisons and the assumption that something *new* was happening in the GDR were somewhat misplaced.

For the reasons already elaborated, it is misleading to imagine 'the independent peace movement' as something directly equivalent to what those words might mean in a Western context. To talk of *'the . . . movement'* suggests a degree of cohesion and organisation that is simply not possible and does not exist in the GDR. Western peace movements, fragmented though they often are, tend to be held together by well-publicised public meetings and demonstrations, by newsletters, magazines, and books, by articles in—and letters to—the local and national press, by coverage on radio and television, and by the existence of umbrella organisations such as CND that speak for them and co-ordinate their activities. Such possibilities are simply not open to independent initiatives in Socialist states. There are no independent campaigns that one can 'join' by paying an annual subscription, and unofficial gatherings—when they do occur—are typically small, quiet, and careful, sensitively

22

feeling out the boundaries of the permissible with an instinct peculiar to those who have known the 'system' from birth. Their contacts are by word of mouth, via a well-developed 'grapevine'; their information comes from the acquired skill of reading between the lines of official and Church publications; and reports of their successes and failures reach them—in the GDR at least—from the news bulletins and current affairs programmes of West German television.

There are no 'leading personalities' in the autonomous peace movement: there is no apparatus—nor for that matter the need or desire—for them to emerge. Some names are well-known: names from within the Church, names of a handful of critical writers and intellectuals, though many of those have long since departed to the West. But it is above all a spontaneous movement of anonymous young people, and the reasons for that are as familiar in the GDR as they are in the West. Conformism is at a premium in East German schools, yet the mannerisms, the tastes in music, the hairstyles and habits of dress—especially in the shape of that all-German teenage garment, the parka—are often barely distinguishable from those of young West Germans. Like young West Germans they know that the world they will inherit from their parents is in a mess, that a new arms race threatens their very survival, and that—in the case of the boys—they will soon be drafted into the army. There have at times been spectacular confrontations between young people and the authorities, including what amounted to a riot at a rock concert celebrating the anniversary of the founding of the Republic on 7 October 1977 on the Alexanderplatz in the heart of East Berlin: violence continued until well into the night, and there were persistent—though unconfirmed—reports that some police were killed.

Such events are exceptional, though perhaps symptomatic of a bottled-up resentment that is far from being an East German speciality. What *is* new, and what has put new vigour into the autonomous peace movement is first the widespread knowledge of the flowering of the Western peace movements, reported not only on West German television, but given saturation coverage in the East German media, and second the dawning of a new, sceptical anti-

or post-materialist mood among the young. The reward for conformism in the GDR has traditionally been access to higher education and a 'decent' career. For many, that prospect does not have the same appeal that it used to, which means that more and more young people find the incentive to conform less compelling, and the sanctions against non-conformity—experienced by their parents in the much more oppressive fascist and Stalinist eras—that much less daunting.

3

ISSUES

The issues that have been taken up by the autonomous peace movement in the GDR are not the same ones that have most exercised the new peace movements of Western Europe. The almost exclusive concentration on nuclear weapons that is characteristic of much Western campaigning has in the GDR for over thirty years been much more a feature of the 'official' peace movement's activities. It is only recently that a certain convergence with the major concerns of the Western peace movements has occurred at the 'unofficial' level in the GDR. Thus the annual Report of the Church Leadership, delivered in September 1982, analysed at length the strategy of 'deterrence', which it dismissed as 'a misuse of the right to self-defence that every country has', proposing in its place a 'categorical imperative for disarmament': 'Arm only in such a way that the other side can copy it exactly without making you feel threatened!' (*Frankfurter Rundschau,* 18 October 1982). The Report also proposed the establishment of nuclear-free zones in Europe, and discussed the issue of pacifism—a topic of particular delicacy in Eastern Europe, where pacifism is officially condemned for its failure to take sides, and rejected as unnecessary in the 'peace state'.

For a long time, though, debate at the grassroots level in the GDR has been focused on matters that a superficial Western eye could all too easily dismiss as provincial. Yet these are issues that in an East German context are of immediate importance: issues where the peace movement may hope for some tangible success, and issues that at the same time involve the creation of that vital 'space' that the peace movement needs to function in. And they *are* 'issues': to talk of them as 'demands' would again be to fall into the trap of seeing what is happening in the GDR in terms of the way these things are done in the West.

25

The main ones fall broadly into two categories. The first group centres on the problem of *military service,* and involves in particular proposals for a 'community peace service' as an alternative to conscription, to service as a 'construction soldier' (see below), and to service in the reserves. The second group is concerned with what is seen as the growing *militarisation of everyday life,* as exemplified in the recent introduction of yet more pre-military training for school-children, the intensification of civil-defence exercises, the prominence of war toys in shops and public nurseries, and the general propagation of a crude 'friend/foe' mentality in public attitudes towards the West.

A third general issue is the extent to which the GDR can make *unilateral gestures* to help lower both tension and the level of armaments. And intimately bound up with all of these is a fourth issue, for a long time only implicit, but of late becoming increasingly explicit: the issue of *human rights and civil liberties*—of the right of the peace movement to gather, to speak out openly and without fear of reprisal, of the right of access to the information and ideas that it needs, and of the right to meet, discuss, and act together with members of the peace movements of other countries.

Conscription and 'Community Peace Service'

When the two German states were founded in 1949, wide-spread domestic revulsion against all forms of militarism together with an international wariness of 'the Germans' ensured that neither of them had an army. The congruence of this anti-militarist policy with the philosophy of the SED was reflected in its declaration at the time that 'Never again shall a German pick up a weapon'. The Americans at least were already becoming aware of the strategic importance of West Germany in the newly divided Europe, and in 1956, in the face of massive popular disapproval, conscription was introduced in the Federal Republic. In the GDR para-military police units had been formed in 1952, and West German rearmament provided the pretext for turning these at the beginning of 1956 into a fully-fledged army, the 'National

26

People's Army' ('Nationale Volksarmee', or 'NVA'), integrated into the newly-formed Warsaw Pact. The NVA, however, unlike the West German Bundeswehr, was a volunteer army. Much pressure was exerted on potential recruits by the Party, the unions, and above all the Free German Youth organisation, and a new clause was added to the Constitution declaring that 'Service for the protection of the homeland and the achievements of the working people is an honourable national duty of the citizens of the German Democratic Republic'.

All, however, to little avail. A major practical objection to remedying the situation by introducing conscription was the fear that this might encourage even more young people to flee to the West—the People's Chamber had, after all, in March 1955 passed a resolution 'For the Protection of the Peace-Loving Youth of West Germany' offering asylum to young people seeking to avoid the impending threat of conscription to *that* country's army. On 13 August 1961 the border to the West was finally sealed as work began on the construction of the Berlin Wall. On 24 January 1962 a Conscription Law ('Wehrpflichtgesetz') was passed, providing for the call-up of all able-bodied citizens between the ages of 18 and 50; a minimum of 18 months military service was to be the norm for all young men.

Unlike the West German conscription law, the new East German one contained no provision for conscientious objection. Partly because of the national guilty conscience about the German past, and partly to counter the daunting groundswell of public opinion against rearmament, the West Germans had, and still have, one of the most liberal approaches to conscientious objection in the world. Their Constitution had after all from the outset proclaimed that 'No-one may be obliged against his conscience to perform armed military service'. The nearest equivalent provision in the East German Constitution stated that 'No citizen may participate in military activities that serve the suppression of a people'. The problem was that the 'Socialism equals Peace' theory meant that objecting to military service in the GDR must by definition mean objecting to peace. There is, according to this line of thought, a world of difference between con-

27

scription in the West and conscription in the East:

> In the imperialist states universal conscription is used to create mass armies that are prepared for aggression; in the Socialist countries it is seen as the most effective way of ensuring the necessary personnel for a modern army ready for action to ward off acts of imperialist aggression.
>
> *(Kleines Politisches Wörterbuch,* 1000)

And for this reason, the East Berlin *Berliner Zeitung* had, on 24 January 1962—the day the Conscription Law was published—informed its readers:

> We support all young people in West Germany who refuse military service, for they are weakening NATO's imperialist army. In the GDR there can and will be no refusal of military service, for we are protecting peace and Socialism.
>
> (Quoted in Eisenfeld, 41)

Notwithstanding the authorities' forceful propaganda campaign against potential refusers, not everyone saw it this way, and some young men did refuse to serve in the new conscript People's Army. The punishment for refusal was imprisonment, and some went to prison; in general though the authorities, wary of stirring up a hornets' nest, acted with circumspect indulgence: it has been estimated that out of a probable total of around 3,000 conscientious objectors in the first full year of conscription, less than a dozen ended up in prison (Eisenfeld, 48 and 69).

The introduction of conscription in January 1962 was, more than any other single factor, the issue that led to the birth of a recognisably autonomous, critical peace movement in the GDR: conscription and conscientious objection remain to this day one of its main concerns. The Protestant Church had been troubled by the ethics of the matter long before 1962, and it accordingly took up with the authorities the cause of the young men who found themselves falling foul of the new law. The result was that on 7 September 1964 the National Security Council passed a decree amending the Conscription Law to provide for the establishment of 'Con-

28

struction Units' in the army (see Documents). 'Construction Soldiers' ('Bausoldaten') would not be required to engage in armed service, but would instead be involved in building military and other installations, in making good damage resulting from military exercises, and in rescue operations in the case of natural disasters.

The Bausoldaten Decree looked like an important concession: no other Warsaw Pact country had—or has—permitted such a degree of absolution from military service. The State, however, painted matters in different terms: there was in any case an urgent need to construct military installations, and the Bausoldaten could thus be represented not as people who had opted out of military service, but as those who were fulfilling their 'rights and obligations' in a different way. The decree was thus officially presented as a means of

> enabling every citizen—including those who for genuine reasons of conscience have not yet appreciated that armed service is service in the cause of peace—to avail himself of his civic rights and meet his civic obligations on the basis of equality of rights and respect.
>
> (Quoted in Eisenfeld, 66)

The Bausoldaten Decree did not meet the wishes of those calling for an alternative to military service. Bausoldaten were still uniformed *army* units, and subject to army discipline and the command of army officers. Unlike other soldiers, they were not required to swear an 'oath' ('Eid'); nonetheless, a 'promise' ('Gelöbnis') was required of them that included the obligation to

> contribute actively to ensuring that the National People's Army, alongside the Soviet Army and the armies of our Socialist allies, can protect the Socialist state against all enemies and achieve victory.

The requirements for becoming a Basuoldat are very liberal: 'religious views or similar grounds' are the sole criterion, but practice has shown that the *possibility* of this alternative form of military service has generally been kept very quiet: throughout the sixties and much of the seventies many young East Germans seem to have been quite unaware of it. Only

29

recently, not least because of publicity on West German television, has it become more widely known—and the number of Bausoldaten has significantly increased. Something else that was not immediately apparent, but soon became so, was that to have been a Bausoldat means a black mark in the files that are kept on every East German: access to further and higher education, as well as to many careers, turns out to be difficult, if not impossible, for most ex-Bausoldaten.

Since 1964 three possibilities have been open to young East Germans faced with call-up. The one opted for by the vast majority is to do the eighteen months of basic military service—though those wishing to go on to higher education are normally expected to 'volunteer' for a further one and a half years. The second possibility is to apply to become a Bausoldat (which frequently involves a delay in drafting until around the age of 25): it has been estimated, in the absence of official statistics, that throughout the sixties and seventies an average of 500 young men per year took this option, though only about half of them are eventually drafted (Eisenfeld, 71). (By way of comparison, in West Germany the numbers of recognised conscientious objectors averaged two to three thousand per year in the early sixties, and then climbed to over thirty thousand by the end of the seventies.) The third possibility is to refuse call-up completely. These 'absolute refusers' ('Totalverweigerer') probably total around 200 per year, of whom about half are Jehovah's Witnesses (Eisenfeld, 72f.). The punishment for 'absolute refusal' is at least 18 months, and sometimes as much as 26 months, in prison: the authorities do not, however, always press the matter, and Totalverweigerer may find themselves simply classified as 'unfit for service', and let off with a very big black mark on their files.

The reaction of the Protestant Church to the new situation was singularly outspoken: unlike the West German Church, which still talks in a mealy-mouthed way about armed service and conscientious objection *both* being ways of 'serving peace', the East German Church produced in 1965 a lengthy 'Recommendation for the Pastoral Care of Conscripts' which, while acknowledging the State's need for security, explicitly recognised that Bausoldaten and Totalverweigerer

30

were giving more profound expression to their witness for peace than those who had accepted normal conscription:

> It cannot be said that the Church's witness for peace manifests itself with equal clarity in all three of these decisions that young Christians in the GDR take today. It is much more the case that those who refuse conscription, and pay in suffering with loss of personal liberty in the penal camp for their obedience, and also Bausoldaten, who take upon themselves the interminable burden of questions of conscience and decision, testify more clearly to our Lord's present-day commandment of peace.
>
> (Quoted in Büscher et al., 22f.)

The authorities were furious. The Church's Recommendation was pronounced 'hostile to the State'. The Church did not retract the Recommendation, and in theory it has remained valid ever since, though care has been taken to give it little further publicity. The Church continued to offer some support and help to Bausoldaten and Totalverweigerer, but in general they found themselves left more to their own devices for much of the rest of the sixties. By the early seventies a mood of near despair had set in among many of those pressing for proper recognition of conscientious objection, alleviated somewhat in 1975 when it became apparent that the authorities were now going to employ Bausoldaten on work of a less military—and some cases even civilian—nature. But all the time the number of *ex*-Bausoldaten was steadily increasing. They kept in touch with one another, discussed problems of peace, and even began, within the framework of the Church, to organise regular seminars—most notably in the Saxon village of Königswalde, where 'Peace Seminars' attracting upwards of a hundred people, many of them former Bausoldaten, have now been held regularly at six-monthly intervals since 1972. Bausoldaten remain one of the most coherent elements in the autonomous peace movement, for, as a recent West Germany study points out:

> Involuntarily the SED set up a clearly visible little piece of peace movement, for in the Construction Units young people are brought together who are inspired by the same idea: not to bear arms, not to kill. As, like all East German soldiers, they are obliged to wear

31

uniform, they can be seen in the streets of towns and villages, in their distinctive uniforms with the spade emblem on the epaulette. Sometimes they meet with abuse, but in the majority of cases they are respected. In sum: a uniform for a division of the peace movement, an East German speciality.

(Die Friedensbewegung in der DDR, published by the
Friedrich-Ebert-Stiftung, Bonn 1982, 19)

From the outset the Bausoldaten had been quietly pressing for the institution of a genuine alternative to military service—the possibility of civilian service in hospitals, with old people, children, the handicapped, and in social welfare. (The model is undoubtedly that of the 'community service' undertaken by conscientious objectors in West Germany, though to say so openly would hardly be politic.) The 1975 change in army policy concerning the type of work Bausoldaten do may have been partly a response to this, though it was undoubtedly also occasioned by the fact that the programme of military building—particularly airfields—was by then more or less complete. The issue was not, however, one that excited much debate, even in the churches.

Not, that is, until May 1981, when a group of Christians in Dresden produced a proposal for the People's Chamber to debate the introduction of a 'Community Peace Service' (Sozialer Friedensdienst) as an alternative to conscription (see Documents). (The abbreviation 'SoFd' has since become almost universally familiar, and has led to the coining of the word 'SoFdies' for supporters of the idea.) The proposal, which provided for a twenty-four-month service in order to discourage 'shirkers' from the standard eighteen-month conscription, was presented both as a way of testifying to the desire for peace and as a means of helping to solve the chronic staff shortages in hospitals and the social services. It was taken up with gusto by Christians throughout the country, who in large numbers followed its recommendation to write in to their Churches in support of the proposal. By the end of November 1981 the initiative had been formally welcomed by all eight of the country's Evangelical Church regions. Suddenly, the idea of a Community Peace Service had become a central issue. It remains so still: indeed, the 'SoFd' proposal is probably the most specific and widely-

32

supported single item on the agenda of the autonomous peace movement.

It has, moreover, recently been more explicitly extended to include *reservists,* who, after all, make up the bulk of the adult male population. In 1982 there was a marked increase in the numbers of men called up to do six to twelve weeks training as reservists, and a corresponding increase in the numbers of those who, having done standard military service, had in the meantime decided to refuse further calls to arms. There is no legal provision for this, as Bausoldaten status cannot be granted retroactively: refusal to serve in the reserve means six to eight months in prison. Nineteen eighty-two also saw the passing of a new Conscription Law which introduces a provision for the call-up of women between the ages of eighteen and fifty in states of emergency. This in its turn has provided a focus of attention for women activists in the peace movement: in October 1982 several hundred of them signed a letter to Erich Honecker protesting at the new provisions and raising other peace-related issues (see Documents).

The 'official' peace movement has not found itself able to take the 'SoFd' proposal on board. The authorities' response to the Church proposals has not been encouraging. In a discussion with theology students at the Humboldt University in East Berlin on 12 September 1981 the Secretary of State for Church Affairs, Klaus Gysi, responded in negative terms to a question about the Community Peace Service proposal:

> Peace marches, like the one from Brussels to Paris, exert a certain attraction on young people, and ideas expressed there reach us too. In this way 'SoFd' has—in part—been imported into this country from outside. It's perfectly normal—after the recent Protestant Assembly in Hamburg too—for a proposal such as this to arise here as well. But we can't have it. For a whole series of reasons. The most important are: in our circumstances it would mean abandoning universal conscription. Unlike West Germany and Switzerland we don't investigate the objector's grounds of conscience. If a citizen of our Republic says he cannot in all conscience do armed service, he can become a Bausoldat. . . . There is no question of changing the Constitution and the Law. . . . We have our obligations to the

33

Warsaw Pact . . . that must be kept. Apart from that, military strength is the greatest contribution to securing peace. In any case, 'Social Peace Service'—the phrase would mean that service in the People's Army was 'Anti-Social War Service', and the vast majority of young Christians undertake armed service in the People's Army—we can't slander them. The bishops have also clearly recognised that, also that this would be interfering with the State's most inherent right. The Bausoldaten arrangement has proved perfectly satisfactory here, and we see no reason to depart from it. Anyone who doesn't accept the State's unambiguous position on this is simply showing that he is out to seek confrontation.

(Quoted in Büscher et al., 174f.)

A couple of months later, Werner Walde, Secretary of the Cottbus district of the SED, put the State's view of the matter much more pithily: 'These people', he said, referring to the 'SoFdies', 'forget that our whole Republic is Community Peace Service' (ibid., 33).

Militarisation and 'Education For Peace'

The military and ideological threat that the capitalist countries pose has always been acutely felt in the Communist world. At the end of the Second World War the military threat was perceived to derive in particular from the Americans' sole possession of the atomic bomb. The response from the East was massive world-wide propaganda campaigns, of the type conducted by the World Peace Council, to have the Bomb banned. The peace campaigns have continued, but the steady increase in Soviet power, and not least its own acquisition of nuclear weapons, have meant that they have been increasingly accompanied by a more and more thorough militarisation of society in Eastern Europe. This has been nowhere more true than in the GDR. The combination of 'olive branch' and 'big stick' as the twin instruments of foreign policy is familiar enough in the West as well, where it is closely associated with the official strategy of 'deterrence'. The assumption that if we keep up the pressure for long enough the 'other side' will start to crumble of its own accord and we will then have it all our own way is also a primary article of faith in much Western strategic thinking, though often it is implicit rather than explicit. Eastern thinking, informed by the assurance of the inevitable ultimate emergence of world-wide Communism, is more open: the principle of 'peaceful coexistence' presupposes an ever-intensified world-wide ideological struggle, the success of which is ensured by the immense—but nonetheless purely *defensive*—military might of the ever-expanding Socialist bloc.

This philosophy forms the basis of East German military thinking. The following words of the GDR's Minister of Defence and leading exponent of Marxist-Leninist military thinking, General Heinz Hoffmann, illustrate it well:

We Communists know, as Rosa Luxemburg so strikingly put it, that 'down here in the real world a state of eternal peace, of the type envisaged by the greatest German writers and philosophers, like Kant for instance, is not possible until capitalism is eradicated root and branch'. But humankind does not need to wait until the last bastion of capitalism has fallen, until our world is Communist. Since 1917 the Leninist policy of 'peaceful coexistence' has shown the way to a solution of the problem of peace. And with the coming into being and flourishing of the Socialist community of states and their joint military might, the material guarantees for the realisation of this solution have been created and increased. This will remain so until the day when the weapons are knocked from the hands of the enemies of Socialism for once and for all! With this earnest determination to strike back if necessary with all the harshness at our disposal, the members of the Allied Forces—among them the soldiers of the National People's Army—are prepared for the wars that are still possible, so that their Socialist homeland may blossom in peace and happiness. This is the logical conclusion of real, Socialist humanism. A humanism that, as Heinrich Mann once said, knows how to look after itself, and knows no weakening in the face of its murderers.

(*Einheit*—theoretical organ of the SED—Number 3, 1976)

Since the price of Socialism is eternal vigilance, and since this eternal vigilance must take the form of military preparedness, the GDR has put an immense effort into ensuring not only that a conventional standing army is maintained, but that every citizen is thoroughly versed in both the theory and

35

the practice of armed defence. At the theoretical level this involves above all the inculcation of a clear and 'correct' 'friend/foe' attitude. The theory of the 'Feindbild'—of the 'image of the enemy'—receives much attention in the GDR, and its application in real life means instilling an unambiguous attitude of *love* for the 'friends' of Socialism—the working people of the GDR, the Soviet Union, and the other Socialist states—and of *hatred* for its enemies—the imperialist and war-mongering West. Only thus can the necessary motivation be generated for the selfless devotion to the military protection of the fatherland that is required of all citizens. (It must not be forgotten that the people of the GDR—unlike those of most other European countries—do not have a historical national identity: 'patriotism' as a motive for defending the country, above and beyond the given political order, cannot therefore be taken for granted by the government. The credibility of the 'Feindbild' is in any case regularly subverted for many East Germans by their contacts with friends and relations from the West.)

In the words—once again—of General Hoffmann: 'Anyone who cannot love something properly will not be able to hate his enemies properly; he could fight against anyone—or against no-one' (H. Hoffmann, *Sozialistische Landesverteidigung,* vol. 3, Berlin 1974, 384). Elsewhere, Hoffmann has described the appropriate attitude to 'friends' and 'enemies': 'To our friend we give all our love and our absolute personal dedication. Against the enemy—who has not shrunk from any crime or bestiality—we direct our abhorrence and contempt' (ibid., 317). The theory of the 'Feindbild' is not just a speciality of the singularly forthright General Hoffmann. Erich Honecker too has made it clear that 'We have every reason to maintain our eternal vigilance both politically and militarily. Our image of the enemy is absolutely right. It doesn't need changing in the least, because the enemy himself hasn't changed' (E. Honecker, *Reden und Aufsätze,* vol. 1, Berlin 1975, 439).

The 'Feindbild' of the GDR is directed in particular at West Germany, and especially at those forces that wish to destroy the achievements of Socialism: the industrialists, the exiled former landowners, the military. The fortified border between the two states—which is also the frontier between the systems—is portrayed in the West as a device for keeping the East Germans *in*; in the GDR it is the means of keeping these hostile forces *out*. The stronger and more impenetrable it is the better, and the brave men who guard it are 'our' first line of defence against 'them' out there.

These ideas are inculcated into young East Germans from the very beginning of the education system. According to paragraph five of the 1982 Conscription Law, 'Preparation for military service forms an integral part of education in schools, vocational institutions, technical colleges, and universities and other institutions of higher education.' In the very first school year (at the age of six) the standard curriculum already includes a visit to the classroom from a soldier of the National People's Army, a visit that is preceded and followed by carefully guided discussion about the role of the Army in protecting peace and the homeland. Even before children go to school these ideas and feelings will have been promoted through the war toys that—after being banned in 1945 and since reintroduced as 'patriotic toys'— are on sale everywhere in the GDR (just as in the West), and are widely used in the nurseries and kindergartens that virtually all pre-school children in the country attend. The 'friend/foe' mentality, and the image of the soldier as the people's friend and guardian, are obligatory elements in the following years of the school curriculum, which also provides for further contacts with Army personnel. As the children get older, the discussion becomes less purely emotive and more theoretical, and at the same time elements of practical training for the Army and civil defence are introduced.

Military education and training is not confined to the schools. Nearly all East German children between the ages of six and fourteen belong to the 'Pioneer' organisation, whose activities in any case are closely tied in with the school system. Here too, military thinking is paramount: there are military-style camps, games, and competitions, and each Pioneer group is 'twinned' with an Army company. At the age of fifteen, most children join the Free German Youth (FDJ), where the propaganda and training continue. Membership of the FDJ continues until the age of twenty-five, but in the meantime from the age of seventeen onwards two-year part-time paramilitary training courses are available under the aegis of the 'Society for Sport and Technology' (GST). The courses are deliberately designed to be exciting for young people, and include sailing, flying, parachuting, and also the much sought-after possibility of passing the driving test. They also include military-style manoeuvres and weapons training. They are to all intents and purposes an obligatory part of the senior school curriculum, as well as of vocational courses: more than ninety per cent of young people undertake them, with the result that by the time they join the Army, East German recruits are already exceptionally well-versed in the ins and outs of military life—which makes things much easier for the Army's training officers.

After leaving the Army, East Germans are placed in the Reserve until their mid-fifties. Here too, many of them are involved for much of their life in regular courses to keep them up to scratch, and abreast of the latest developments in technology and strategic thinking. Active and committed Party members may also be involved in the 'Working Class Combat Groups' (Kampfgruppen der Arbeiterklasse), which are attached to factories and other places of work. Some 400,000 men are active in this armed militia, whose tasks include internal security in peace time, and back-up support for the Army in case of war. And then finally there is civil defence, which involves all citizens. Whereas the instruction of boys is directed towards service in the Army, girls are normally trained for civil defence work. Since 1 December 1981 participation in civil defence courses has been obligatory for everyone between the ages of 18 and 65, and civil defence exercises involving whole towns in 'protect and survive'-type operations are regularly carried out.

The Churches in the GDR have always found the militarisation of daily life an especially difficult aspect of their society to accommodate to. The determined promotion of the 'Feindbild' in particular, the quite deliberate efforts on the part of the State to instil hatred of the 'enemy', runs directly counter to all Christian notions of 'charity' and 'loving one's enemy'. There is no doubt that this process of militarisation has intensified over the years, and there is no doubt either that it has become an increasingly important means of social control within society. Both of these points were made in a 'Declaration on the Problems of Peace', produced in November 1981 by the Church's Saxony region:

> Many people are beginning to see that the present system of maintaining peace through deterrence no longer makes sense and is no longer acceptable, so that new and different ways must be sought to enable the peoples of this world to live together in peace. . . . We understand, affirm, and support the security interests of our State. But we must give voice to our concern that our whole social life is being increasingly permeated by military aspects: from military parades to the kindergarten, from fenced-off forests to the criteria for admission to educational courses, from the children's war toys to civil defence exercises. None of this serves the real security and future of our country; on the one hand it engenders fear, on the other it accustoms people to the possibility of war; it may be a way of achieving discipline, but it does not help people to work creatively at building peace.
>
> (Quoted in Ehring and Dallwitz, 196f.)

The issue of militarisation first became a really major area of debate in 1978, the year in which the Government introduced a new 'Decree on Defence Studies' (Wehrkundeerlass). This provided for the introduction of both theoretical and practical military courses in the final two years of full-time schooling — in other words for fourteen- to sixteen-year-olds. The introduction of Defence Studies, which took place in the new school year in the autumn of 1978, meant, in purely quantitative terms, a relatively minor addition to the amount of military instruction that schoolchildren already received. It was, however, significant in that military preparedness was now also to be taught as a subject in its own right: previously these matters had been integrated into the teaching of other subjects, in particular history, social studies, and sport. Of even more importance, as it turned out, was the popular reaction to the new Decree: it, more than anything else, was the factor that really awakened the new autonomous peace movement in the GDR.

Some two years before the rebirth of the Western peace movements, a flurry of activity was already being generated

39

in the GDR by the rumours that, early in 1978, were beginning to circulate about Government plans to introduce Defence Studies. By the spring the rumours were confirmed; in the summer the Decree was duly passed; and in the autumn the courses became part of the school syllabus. Objections to the proposal were voiced both by the Churches and by individuals: it is in the GDR the right of every citizen to petition the authorities, and to expect his or her petition to be duly considered and replied to. To exercise this right where it involves a contentious matter can require courage; many parents did submit petitions ('Eingaben') expressing their concern. The replies they got were not encouraging, and in the event their expressions of concern turned out to have been of no avail.

The Church's reaction was more public. It was clear that the congregations were very worried, and their concern was duly passed on formally to the State authorities, together with the proposal that at least an element of Peace Studies be included in the new courses—once again to no avail. More importantly in the long term for the autonomous peace movement, the Federation of Evangelical Churches decided to counter the introduction of Defence Studies with its own programme of 'Education for Peace'. The idea was not new—a model Peace Studies seminar had already been developed in 1974—but the Government had now given it a new urgency. In July 1978 the Conference of Evangelical Churches resolved to initiate a programme of study and action in Peace Education, which resulted in September 1980 in the publication of a wide-ranging document setting out guidelines and principles—a document that laid especial stress on the need to counter the 'friend/foe' schema, and on practising non-aggression at the most immediate level in the family and with one's fellow beings.

Meanwhile, in September 1979, on the fortieth anniversary of the outbreak of the Second World War, in churches throughout both the Germanies, a 'Statement on Peace' was read out:

We know that long before a war breaks out it has already begun in the hearts and minds of the people; mistrust and fear and the sense of threat extinguish all other hopes. For this reason we must provide more consistently for education for peace.

(Quoted in Ehring and Dallwitz, 45)

It was the first time in ten years that the Evangelical Churches in both East and West Germany had issued a common statement. From now on the two Churches were to cooperate closely in their programme of Peace Education: something that presumably had neither been foreseen nor intended by the East German Government when it drew up its plans for Defence Studies.

Unilateral Gestures

In Britain, 'unilateralism' is a crucial element in the peace movement's demands, and to wear the nuclear disarmament badge is tantamount to proclaiming 'I am a unilateralist'. This fact is often not appreciated by Continental peace campaigners, for whom wearing the CND badge is usually no more than a general declaration of opposition to nuclear weapons—without implying a specific programme for getting rid of them. Equally, supporters of CND do not always appreciate that 'unilateralism' in its British form cannot be simply inserted without more ado into the agenda of Continental peace movements.

This is especially true in the case of the two Germanies, and even more so in the case of East Germany. In the first place, neither of the German states *possesses* nuclear weapons of its own that it could renounce: there is thus no parallel for that particular central aspect of British unilateralism. Second, the CND aim of also requiring *foreign* nuclear weapons to be removed implies national sovereignty of a degree that permits that demand to be made in the first place: both the German states are subject to troop-stationing agreements that in fact limit their sovereignty in this particular area. Third, as far as the GDR is concerned, the country has in any case committed itself to the alliance with the Soviet Union *in its Constitution*, Article Six of which states: 'The German Democratic Republic is allied for all time and irrevocably with the Union of Soviet Socialist Republics.' And then fourth, there is the much debated question of whether there *are* nuclear weapons in the GDR in any case: whereas an estimated five thousand nuclear warheads are housed in *West* Germany, a widespread assumption has it that the Soviet Union stations only the delivery systems on *its* allies' soil, keeping the warheads—in time of peace—behind its own frontiers.

The room for unilateral initiatives over nuclear weapons is thus very limited in the GDR, and it would be wide of the mark to assume that the CND emblem, which is much in evidence at autonomous peace movement gatherings there, has the same specific implications in the GDR as it does in Britain. In fact, as has been suggested, the manifest major concerns of the autonomous peace movement have been very different issues from those that have most exercised CND.

Nonetheless, unilateral initiatives are implicit in the East German Churches' approach to many of the issues they have discussed, as the slogan 'Make Peace without Weapons' indicates. ('Frieden schaffen ohne Waffen'—now a universal slogan of the autonomous peace movement—was adopted by the Church in both Germanies as the motto of the first joint Peace Week, in the autumn of 1980; the slogan clearly proposes a way of keeping the peace that runs directly counter to both States' ideas on the matter.) Proposals for unilateral steps in the specific area of nuclear weapons have been made as well. They originate from what is in effect the Church's 'think tank' on peace policy, the 'Study Group on Peace Affairs' (Studienreferat Friedensfragen) of the 'Theological Studies Division', which in its turn is associated with—though not officially a part of—the Federation of Evangelical Churches. The Study Group, which had been instrumental in the Church's proposals for Peace Education, took part at the beginning of the eighties in discussions with the Dutch Inter-Church Peace Council (IKV) about the Dutch churches' popular unilateralist proposal to 'Help Rid the World of Nuclear Weapons, Starting with the Netherlands'— an initiative that had been warmly welcomed by official circles in the GDR.

42

In March 1981, as a result of these discussions, an ad-hoc committee on disarmament set up by the Study Group produced a 'Statement on the Question of Nuclear Weapons'. The Statement began by reiterating the conclusions the committee had reached in 1980 as a result of its discussions of the Dutch initiative—conclusions that saw no possible moral alternative to 'nuclear pacifism':

> We must publicly renounce the system of nuclear deterrence, and the military and political use of nuclear weapons and other weapons of mass destruction. We declare that we will not take part in a war that is waged with such weapons.
>
> (Quoted in Büscher et al., 127)

The Statement then went on to make a careful but unambiguous proposal for a unilateral initiative by the GDR in one of the few areas where it *could* renounce the use of nuclear weapons:

> In the present European situation, which is characterised by growing crises in the economic and political spheres, and by the continuing lack of progress in arms limitation talks, duly considered unilateral gestures (which must not be allowed to endanger military security) would still seem to be a possible way of setting in motion in Europe a movement that runs counter to the ever-accelerating armament process. We consider that a unilateral renunciation by the GDR—carried out in agreement with its Warsaw Pact allies—of nuclear-capable delivery systems of its own should be aimed for as a step in the direction of the denuclearisation of Europe.
>
> (Ibid., 127f.)

Eight months later, in November 1981, these ideas were taken up by the Saxon regional Synod of the Church. Saxony, the heartland of Pietism, has played a vanguard role in the Church's peace movement, and in the same 'Declaration on the Problems of Peace' in which it voiced its disquiet at the militarisation of everyday life, the Saxon Church became the first of the eight GDR Church regions to propose a unilateral reduction of nuclear weapons. Thanking the American churches for their opposition to American nuclear policy, and the Dutch Reformed Church for its unilateralist proposals, the Declaration went on:

> We cannot support these initiatives simply by applauding them, but only by acting in an equivalent way that is appropriate to our situation. We therefore advocate:
> — duly considered disarmament gestures, in agreement with our allies (for example a reduction in the numbers of SS-20 missiles)
> — defensive, low-threat security systems (for example the elimination of our superiority in numbers of tanks) and thus the rebuilding of trust in Europe from *our* side.
>
> (Quoted in Ehring and Dallwitz, 198)

Civil Liberties

Like unilateralism, the issue of civil liberties is implicit in much that the autonomous peace movement has said and done; only occasionally has it become an explicit and specific theme in its own right. Civil liberties—and in particular the rights of freedom of expression, assembly, and association—are inherent preconditions of any peace movement activity: they imply the essential 'space' within which it can take place. At the same time, curtailment of civil liberties is scarcely conducive to an atmosphere in which peace may flourish if it leads to resentment, disaffection, and tension within the population: a situation that may be further aggravated by being exploited in its turn by 'the other side'. Civil liberties are, in other words, often tantamount to 'peace rights'.

The official conception of 'civil liberties' in the GDR is not the same as the Western interpretation of the term. In the West, civil liberties are seen in the first instance as rights of the isolated individual against the State; in Socialist countries such as the GDR the assumption that the interests of the individual—who is now a fully integrated part of the whole—and the State are now *identical* removes the preconditions for this perspective. Instead, official commentaries on the GDR Constitution emphasise first that what is now guaranteed is the right of citizens to *participate* in the affairs of society, and second that these rights are at one and the

44

same time also *duties* of the citizens:

> It is not freedom *from* society and the State, but freedom *in* Socialist
> society and the Socialist State, all-embracing involvement and
> participation in the affairs of society, that permit the development
> of the Socialist personality and its freedom.
>
> (*Kleines Politisches Wörterbuch,* 578; my italics)

The idea that rights are contained *within* the prescribed
social order is emphasised by the fact that there is in the
GDR no ultimate instance—no Supreme Court or Constitutional Court—to which individuals may appeal if they
feel their civil rights have been infringed. The very existence
of a Socialist system is in itself deemed a sufficient guarantee
that the rights *will* be observed. As Article 86 of the
Constitution puts it:

> Socialist society, the political power of the working people, their
> state and legal order are the fundamental guarantee that the Con-
> stitution will be observed and realised in the spirit of justice,
> equality, fraternity, and humanity.

The demand, frequently raised in the West, that autonomous peace initiatives in Eastern Europe be granted the same
freedom of action that Western peace movements enjoy thus
not only encounters in the East the official objection that
there is no *need* to demonstrate against governments that are
for peace in any case, but also runs up against a fundamentally different conception of civil liberties. The autonomous
peace movement in the GDR is more familiar with the fact
that it is a basic premise of their system that 'bourgeois'
'civil liberties' (which in any case are adjudged hypocritical)
are not appropriate under Socialism, and has accordingly
concentrated more on practical steps to secure the space
within which it can function.

The State's wariness of 'bourgeois' ideas of human rights
and civil liberties is well illustrated by the following anecdote:

> In the early seventies at a May-Day parade in Karl-Marx-Stadt a
> former Bausoldat appeared carrying a banner reading 'For the

45

realisation of human rights!' The State Security officials did not notice what was going on until afterwards when they were sorting through the photographs of the event. The demonstrator was identified, and the banner was—post facto—confiscated.

(Ehring and Dallwitz, 109)

The bold banner-bearer of Karl-Marx-Stadt was not entirely alone. The Helsinki Agreement of 1975, much quoted by the State in the cause both of peace and of its own sovereignty, also gave some impetus to those within the GDR who felt there was room for improvement in the area of civil liberties. Such Church statements as the following indicate the thinking that links these ideas with those of the peace movement:

For this process [of creating and maintaining peace] to continue, steps should be taken to ensure, for example, that the possibilities for people to meet are further developed in both German states. Peace between the states and peace within a society are linked. The ability to deal with, and overcome, conflicts in our daily life and in society, is at the same time a contribution to peace between states, while the repression of conflicts leads to the accumulation of aggressive feelings and to the deflection of these feelings onto an 'enemy'.

(Quoted in Steinweg, 262)

Specific requests from the Church that the State respect the rights of individuals who may not conform have been made in, for instance, the case of Bausoldaten, or of the wearers of the 'Swords into Ploughshares' emblem, and many saw it as a token of a more open engagement for civil liberties that the themes for the Church's 1981 Peace Week should be expressed in a slogan—'Justice—Disarmament—Peace'—that went beyond the more immediate peace issues. It was, however, for some time left to voices that came from outside the Church hierarchy to express what the peace movement really wanted in the area of civil liberties—voices articulated politely but unambiguously in the 'Berlin Appeal':

We propose that the great debate about questions of peace be conducted in an atmosphere of tolerance and recognition of the right of free expression and that every spontaneous public manifesta-

46

tion of the desire for peace should be approved and encouraged.

(See Documents for the full text of the 'Berlin Appeal')

In the course of 1982, similar sentiments began to be expressed more clearly by the Church authorities. In October the Chairman of the Federation of Evangelical Churches, Bishop Werner Krusche, dealt in some detail in his report to the Saxony Synod with the difficulties encountered by pacifists in the GDR. There must, he said, be an 'open dialogue' if non-Marxists were to be able to make their proper contribution to the 'unified peace movement' that the Party made so much of:

> When spontaneous initiatives and grass-roots impetuses that are products of a passion for peace have obstacles put in their way, it doesn't do much for the cause of peace.
>
> (Quoted in *Die Welt,* 1 November 82)

4

EVENTS

The history of the Western peace movements is popularly perceived as the story of a series of *events*: the Aldermaston marches, the demonstrations against the Vietnam war, the recent actions at Comiso and Greenham Common, or the massive rallies in European capitals, in New York, Japan, and elsewhere. In Eastern Europe, spectacular peace rallies, marches, and demonstrations are familiar enough, but they are the exclusive province of the 'official' peace movements, and their demands are directed solely at the West. They have not been, and cannot be, the means by which the autonomous peace movements express themselves. The Church-based peace movement in the GDR has deliberately and carefully avoided spectacular manifestations that might be construed by the authorities as 'opposition': this it has done either by embracing and defusing potentially confrontational activities —as it did with great skill and sensitivity in the case of the Dresden gathering of February 1982—or by judiciously distancing itself from them—as it has done, more contentiously, in the case of the 'Berlin Appeal'.

Rather than initiating large-scale *public* events, the autonomous peace movement in the GDR has concentrated more on discussion and debate, and on the exertion of *discreet* pressure on the authorities where this has been felt necessary and appropriate. It has also, probably much more than the Western peace movements, analysed and sought to practice the virtues of peace at the *inter-personal* level: at home, in the family, among friends, and in the community. This does not mean that there have been no 'events' in the Western sense: there have been, but they are quieter, and much smaller in terms of the numbers present. The difficulty of publicising them, the difficulty of finding a location for them, and the possibility of official discrimination against those known to have participated all ensure that this is so.

And given these circumstances, it is worth bearing in mind that a gathering of a few thousand, or even of a few hundred, in the GDR, or an appeal with 'only' a couple of hundred signatures on it, should not be dismissed as 'insignificant' in the way they might automatically be in the West.

'Events' in the GDR tend to get reported in the Western media (and, via West German television, made common knowledge among the East German population as a whole): that is the case with the four discussed here—the Church 'Peace Weeks', the all-German 'Writers' Gathering' in East Berlin (which, significantly, also received attention in the *East* German media), the launching of the 'Berlin Appeal', and, perhaps the nearest thing in Western eyes to a 'real' event, the Dresden 'Peace Forum'. Between them, they illustrate the range and variety of public manifestations of the autonomous peace movement; but it is essential to appreciate that, although symptomatic, they are not *typical.* The great majority of grass-roots 'events' remain largely unsung: they occur in private homes, in churches, at pop concerts, in small informal gatherings of young people, of certain intellectuals, of ex-Bausoldaten, of the Protestant student organisations—and also, it must never be forgotten, in the hearts and minds of many who take part in 'official' demonstrations.

Peace Weeks

Each autumn since 1980 the Churches in the GDR have organised so-called 'Friedensdekaden': strictly speaking, peace 'decades', where the word has the unusual sense—at least as far as English usage is concerned—of 'a period of ten days'. The first of these ten-day 'weeks' began on 9 November 1980; this day had been chosen by a joint committee of the East and West German Protestant churches for a common 'Rogation Service for the Endangered Peace of the World', the occasion being the opening in Madrid of the Second Conference on European Cooperation and Security. At the suggestion of the Youth Ministry of the East German Church, this was then followed by a 'Friedensdekade',

49

which would end on the Day of Repentence with a service and a minute of remembrance and prayer—a 'Friedensminute'.

The idea of the Peace Week was taken up with enthusiasm by the Church: the motto 'Frieden schaffen ohne Waffen'—'Make Peace without Weapons'—was adopted, and a special bookmarker bearing these words, together with the words 'Swords into Ploughshares' and their now-familiar accompanying emblem, was produced to serve both as an invitation to the week's events, as an aid to discussion and meditation, and as a souvenir. As planned, the week included services and discussions centring on the Christian idea of peace and the ways in which it could be realised in the present-day world. Reports from churches all over the country indicated active and enthusiastic participation by above-average congregations.

Only at the end of the 'Friedensdekade' did the Church get cold feet: in the matter of the planned minute of remembrance and prayer. There were problems in any case in that this 'Friedensminute' would fall in the middle of an ordinary working day. They were compounded by the fact that the appointed time—1 p.m. on Wednesday 19 November—was to be marked throughout the country by the ringing of church bells: this would not have been such a problem were it not for the fact that 1 p.m. on Wednesday 19 November was also the time chosen by the Civil Defence for testing their air-raid sirens. The authorities, learning of the Church's plans, were more than a little alarmed: the contrast between the sirens, symbolising the State's approach to peace, and the bells, symbolising the Church's proposal to 'make peace without weapons', was felt to be at best unfortunate, and at worst provocative. It was even apparently interpreted by some within the Party—with Polish events very much on their minds at the time—as 'a call to a general strike'. In the event, the Church's plan was withdrawn, and the decision as to when to ring the bells for the 'Friedensminute' was left up to individual churches—though with the recommendation that, 'to avoid misunderstandings', 12 noon might be the best time. A few churches nonetheless still braved the sirens and the State and pealed away at one o'clock.

Notwithstanding the little contretemps at the end, the

1980 Peace Week was generally judged a great success, even though the official media kept quite about it, and the Churches decided to repeat the event in 1981. This second 'Friedensdekade' was duly held in both German states from 8 to 18 November, this time under the motto 'Justice—Disarmament —Peace'. As before there were services and discussions, but the range of activities was widened to include 'peace festivals', with poetry, music, and songs. Again there was evidence of interest and enthusiasm—this time not only within the Christian community, but in particular among young people who did not normally form part of the churches' congregations.

By now, peace-week type activities were beginning to 'spill over' from the pre-arranged ten-day period, and the summer of 1982 saw a number of gatherings on church premises, attracting, according to some reports, up to ten thousand young people. Typical of these was the 'Peace Workshop', held at the Church of the Redeemer in an East Berlin suburb on 28 June. Some three thousand people, predominantly young, attended this event, news of which was spread by word of mouth and by cyclostyled leaflets— bearing the obligatory warning 'For Internal Church Use Only'—that invited participants to bring 'instruments, songs, poems, desires, fears and ideas—and a flower in your hair or buttonhole'. In the church itself there were services, dramatic sketches, readings of poetry and prose, music and meditation. Other rooms around the church were set aside for exhibitions and more readings of poetry and prose, many by young people who had indeed followed the invitation and had written down their 'desires, fears and ideas'. Outside in the grounds of the church, walls and trees were covered with posters, photographs, and handwritten texts; pop groups played, a children's corner was set up, and food and drink were on sale. Perhaps most remarkable of all was the 'Speakers' Corner' where anyone and everyone could speak their mind before an attentive crowd of some two or three hundred, a possibility of which many availed themselves, talking openly of their desires for greater freedom of expression in the world outside, and for the State's proclamations of peace to be matched by a demilitarisation of society—yet

51

at the same time expressing due respect for the peace initiatives of the Soviet Union, and avoiding attacks on the basic premises of the Socialist system. Needless to say, the East Berlin 'Peace Workshop' was not mentioned in the East German media; nor were the similar gatherings of 1982. That responsibility was left to the West Germans.

Now that peace movement events are becoming almost routine in East German churches, the 'Peace Week' initiative is beginning to be downstaged somewhat. It remains nonetheless an important focus of debate and activity, and the holding in November 1982 of the third all-German 'Friedensdekade', this time with the theme 'Fear—Trust—Peace', suggests that it is now set fair to become a regular annual event in the calendar of the Churches—and thus of the autonomous peace movement.

The Berlin Writers' Gathering

The weekend of 12–13 December 1981 was a particularly busy one for the East German press. The front pages of the Monday papers on the fourteenth were dominated by three items that could also be expected to make headlines on the West German television news that evening: on the Friday evening Helmut Schmidt had come to the GDR for two days of discussions with Erich Honecker, discussions in which problems of European security loomed especially large; on the Sunday General Jaruzelski had declared a state of emergency in Poland; and as if that was not enough for one weekend, the Sunday evening had also seen the opening speeches of a quite unprecedented two-day gathering of writers from both the Germanies—and beyond—in the grand hall of East Berlin's luxurious Hotel Stadt Berlin.

The invitations to the 'Berlin Gathering for Peace' ('Berliner Begegnung zur Friedensförderung') had been sent out by Stephan Hermlin, a novelist widely respected as one of the more independent spirits in the GDR's intellectual community. (He is also a personal friend of Erich Honecker, and—in the words of the *Guardian*—'a doer of many careful good deeds in private' [29 May 1982].) The joint hosts for the event were the Academy of Arts and the Academy of Sciences of the GDR. Invitations were sent predominantly to writers, but also to scientists, musicians, artists, and academics. About one hundred turned up; most came from the GDR, but a sizeable contingent also came from West Berlin and the Federal Republic, and a handful from other East and West European countries. No attempt had been made to 'doctor' the list: for the first time not only were writers from East and West getting together under the auspices of official East German bodies, but they included among their number distinctly 'uncomfortable' figures such as Hermlin himself, as well as those—like Stefan Heym—who had been expelled from the Writers' Union and prevented from publishing in the East, and others too, who, as guests of the Academies, were making their first visits 'home' again after going into exile in the West.

These facts alone made the Berlin Gathering into a unique occasion. The contributions made to the discussions were frank, though on the whole predictable. There was much vague agreement on the need for trust and understanding—very much the central theme of the event. But when the question of autonomous peace initiatives in the GDR raised its head, as it did on numerous occasions, the participants quickly divided into a spectrum of approaches that ranged from the sizeable group of loyal Party members insisting on the 'no need to demonstrate against our peace-loving Government' line to sceptical West Germans like Günter Grass, who were not at all convinced that grass-roots initiatives were being allowed to flourish as they would have liked.

The most interesting contributions came from the more sceptical and critical East German writers, who made it clear that the country's intellectual community is by no means as monolithic as it is sometimes painted by outsiders. Some, like Rolf Schneider, addressed specific issues head-on:

In East German newspapers you can read, and in East German schools you have to learn, that 'peace has got to be armed'. I consider this statement questionable. I see it as a piece of mental arms race.

Anyone who says 'weapons' is thinking of handling them. Anyone who handles weapons is thinking of war as a possibility—a

53

defensive war may be, but people get killed in those too, and nuclear weapons can be exploded in them. The path that leads from the armed frontier incident to the nuclear blast is a short one.

(Berliner Begegnung, 108)

Volker Braun perceived the State's method of keeping the peace as the cause of much that was wrong with Socialism in the GDR; it demanded, he said, a constant exertion, 'in the pursuit of which Socialism is apt to lose sight of its purpose', and went on to talk of

> the repressive structures that this peace requires, the supreme command over people that this peace requires, the monopoly of information that this peace requires. Peace as an excuse for an utterly unchangeable Socialism, for this world that is galloping along towards nothing better. And I'm supposed to sing its praises! I'm supposed to want it. This peace. And it's not even as if having it this way makes this peace any safer. On the contrary, because we've got it this way, the danger grows that humankind will destroy itself.

(Ibid., 160)

Others spoke of the need for unilateral gestures. Stephan Hermlin even came up with a hitherto unremarked observation from Lenin on the subject—a statement, made in 1917, that had only just been republished:

> Militarism has been able to survive up to now because each side has declared itself ready to disarm if and when its neighbour does so; it—militarism—will disappear when one of the powers disarms first, and the others, sooner or later, follow its example.

(Ibid., 38; Hermlin had come across the quotation in *Beiträge zur Geschichte der Arbeiterbewegung,* Number 3, 1981)

Günter de Bruyn, echoing Volker Braun's remarks, was able to see unilateralism not only as an expedient for breaking the vicious circle of the arms race, but as a way also of reinforcing the State's security. The only way to break the 'deadly spiral' was for someone to leave it, and thereby

> show themselves to be not only braver and morally superior, but

54

they also prove, as the proverb has it, that 'the wiser man gives in';
for the only lasting guarantee of a state's security is a contented
population, and there's little hope of that when it takes its defences
to such an extreme that it devours the very thing that's supposed
to be defended.

(Berliner Begegnung, 81f.)

It was also Günter de Bruyn, one of the GDR's leading
novelists, who spoke most directly and forthrightly about the
need to accept and encourage grass-roots initiatives in the
East German peace movement:

Gratifying as the support may be that the GDR gives to the West
European peace movement, the value of this will remain questionable so long as the impression cannot be avoided that what is
applauded over there is unwelcome over here. The GDR's policies,
aiming at peace and seeking an alliance with peace movements all
over the world, cannot but be vitiated by a refusal to accept the
offer of alliance that comes from independent peace movements in
their own country—like that of young Christians demanding 'community peace service'. If they are pushed off into the underground,
then not only do you lose valuable forces for peace, but you damage
your own credibility. What a bonus it would be, though, if support
for proposals to ban the bomb could also come from an independent
East German peace movement. There is no doubt it would add
weight to the GDR's efforts for peace. It would be nice to think
that this gathering could stimulate some sort of opening here,
though I have to admit I don't hold much hope for it.

(Ibid., 82)

A different approach was suggested by Christa Wolf. When
called upon to speak, she made it clear in her opening remarks
that she did not consider it a coincidence that in the entire
gathering there were only six women present:

I almost wish my turn hadn't come. Then it would have been even
clearer than it already is that the topic we're discussing today is
men's business. I'm convinced of that.

(Ibid., 116)

'We've really got to appreciate', she continued later, 'what the inevitable result is when half of the people who live in a culture are by nature excluded from the things it creates— not even getting in the way when this culture plans its own downfall' (Ibid., 118). Christa Wolf's words gave a feminist twist to an ecological argument that is becoming more and more perceptible in peace movement thinking in the GDR: what women had had no part in was the process of *industrialisation.*

> These missiles and bombs have come into being as the clearest and most distinctive expression of the alienation syndrome of industrial societies which, with their 'faster, better, and more' have subordinated all other values to this 'value' of efficiency; which have forced the mass of people to live hollow lives devoid of reality, and have above all made the natural sciences their servants.
>
> (Ibid., 118)

Christa Wolf's address was the most eloquent of the whole gathering, and her definition of what our society lacks was to be much quoted afterwards:

> We lack things that cannot be measured, things that cannot be seen. . . . We lack friendliness, graciousness, air to breathe, tones to hear, dignity and poetry, trust, spontaneity too. We lack all the things that are the first to go in the kind of atmosphere that descends, and now so oppresses us all in these pre-war times.
>
> (Ibid., 119)

Her personal response would, she pledged, be the only one possible: to write critically of her society, to make it aware of 'what could help it to live and to survive'. 'I can say,' she concluded, 'that I am not going to let anyone at all stop me from doing that' (ibid.).

The Berlin Writers' Gathering provided an unprecedentedly prestigious forum for some remarkably critical speeches by eminent East Germans. The media, Eastern and Western, were present in force. What they reported was less surprising, though: in the East, only the remarks that backed the State's policies were picked up, while the Western media focused on anything and everything that could be construed as evidence of 'dissidence'. The GDR Academy of Arts nonetheless published—as had been agreed in advance—a full verbatim account of the proceedings: the print-run of three thousand copies was very quickly sold out.

Noteworthy though it was, the Berlin Writers' Gathering was not greeted with wholehearted acclamation by grass-roots peace campaigners. Some saw it as a kind of shop window, a deceptive display of freedom of opinion and expression that did not reflect the reality that *they* experienced. There was talk of 'privileged elites' with untypical 'leave to speak and travel'. And travel the writers certainly did: in the last week of May 1982 they gathered again in The Hague, this time at the invitation of Bernt Engelmann, the Chairman of the West German Writers' Union and initiator of the 'European Writers' Appeal' (which was co-sponsored by his East German counterpart Hermann Kant); scarcely a month later they were in Cologne as guests of the Writers' Union itself, and a further meeting was to follow in Sofia. Such officially condoned meetings outside the GDR cannot be accounted activities of the GDR's 'autonomous peace movement', though they continue to be noteworthy for the outspokenness of some of the East German participants. Stephan Hermlin in particular has now spoken out a number of times on behalf of autonomous peace initiatives, whilst remaining a prominent and 'respectable' member of the GDR's literary establishment.

At their meeting in The Hague, the writers issued a unanimous resolution that pledged support to 'all attempts to ensure peace through disarmament, whether or not they have the blessing of the governments in question'. 'We see it as our duty', it continued, 'to help to the best of our ability those who are persecuted for taking up the cause of peace.' And then, as much to their own surprise as to that of the world at large, they concluded their resolution with a proposal, initiated by the Vice-Chairman of the Russian Writers' Association, urging that 'simultaneously and without reservations the two military blocs should be dissolved'. (Quoted in Engelmann, et al., 134)

Havemann, Eppelmann, and the 'Berlin Appeal'

A number of speakers from both East and West had proposed at the Berlin Writers' Gathering that an independent peace movement be given room to develop in the GDR. Little more than a month later the Western media were alerted to what many of them presented as the first real manifestation of just such a movement. On 25 January 1982 an appeal was launched in East Berlin that not only embraced the now familiar concerns of the Church, but touched on other, more contentious matters such as the 'German Problem', and, moreover, invited sympathisers and supporters to add their signatures to the appended list—and that in a country where the organisation of public petitions is illegal unless officially sanctioned.

The 'Berlin Appeal' was formulated jointly by one of the best-known of the GDR's critical Marxists, Robert Havemann, and an East Berlin pastor specialising in work among young people, Rainer Eppelmann. Havemann, born in 1910, had become a member of the Communist Party in 1932; imprisoned and condemned to death by the Nazis, he was released at the end of the war, and after an initial period in West Berlin he took an active and prominent part in the establishment of the GDR as a leading Party functionary, a member of the People's Chamber, a professor of chemistry at the East Berlin Humboldt University, and a founder member of the GDR's Peace Council (his campaigning against the American hydrogen bomb had in the meantime brought him a brief spell of imprisonment in West Berlin, where he was working at the Max Planck Institute). In the 1960s, however, his increasingly unorthodox writings and lectures brought him official disfavour, and he was relieved of his positions, titles, and public awards. Enveloped from now on by official silence in the East, he was adopted in the West as one of the GDR's major 'dissidents'. One thing, though, still stood him in comparatively good stead, and that was the gratitude and respect of one of his former fellow-prisoners from the Nazi years—Erich Honecker. Havemann, unlike some other 'dissidents', was not imprisoned, nor was he exiled to the West: instead he spent some time under house arrest, though this restriction was lifted in the last couple of years of his life. To the end he insisted that the GDR, having laid the foundations of Socialism, was, for all its shortcomings, still the more advanced and 'better German state'. Robert Havemann died on 9 April 1982.

Though virtually unheard in his own country, Havemann became in the last years of his life a significant voice for peace. His approach, however, differed fundamentally from that of the Church-based initiatives: instead of focusing on the immediate, everyday issues, Havemann was more concerned with European and global politics. In particular he was exercised by the fact that the two Germanies had been turned into nothing short of armed military bases by the two superpowers, and that any future war would be fought above all in central Europe. His proposed solution was ambitious but simple: the Soviet Union and the United States should withdraw from their respective halves of Germany, and the two German states should be neutralised and demilitarised, thereby forming the nucleus of an atomic-weapons-free Europe.

These ideas of Havemann's found their way to Western Europe in a series of articles and open letters. Thus in an article in the West German weekly *Die Zeit* in December 1979—five days before the NATO Cruise and Pershing II decision, and a couple of months after Brezhnev had announced the unilateral withdrawal of twenty thousand troops and a thousand tanks from the GDR—he called for the removal of *all* Soviet forces from the GDR, 'if at the same time the USA is prepared for its part too to withdraw *all* its troops, tanks, planes, and other war equipment from the Federal Republic' (*Die Zeit,* 7 December 1979). In June 1981, in an open letter to Helmut Schmidt, whom he called upon to act 'not as a Chancellor of the Americans, but as a Chancellor of the Germans', he proposed the 'step-by-step removal of all nuclear weapons from the territory of the two German states, the withdrawal of the foreign occupation forces from both parts of Germany, demilitarisation and neutralisation of Germany (quoted in Ehring and Dallwitz, 208).

The most prominent of Havemann's appeals was to come

in the autumn of 1981 in the form of an open letter to Leonid Brezhnev, to be presented to the Soviet leader on the occasion of his visit to Bonn in late November (see Documents). The 'Havemann Initiative', as it became known, once more proposed that the key to European peace lay in the demilitarisation and neutralisation of Germany—a process which, he reminded Brezhnev, had been advocated by the Soviet Union itself on various occasions in the post-war years, and which now was dependent on the Soviet Union's willingness to sign the still outstanding peace treaty with Germany. The open letter initially bore twenty-seven East German signatures, headed by that of Robert Havemann, and including that of Rainer Eppelmann. By the time it was delivered to Brezhnev two months later, over two hundred further signatures had been collected in the GDR. These were joined, however, by twenty thousand West German signatories, including many prominent figures in the arts, politics, and the sciences—for the 'Havemann Initiative', now styled as an 'All-German Peace Initiative', had in the meantime been vigorously canvassed throughout the Federal Republic and West Berlin by individuals and groups active in the Western peace movement.

What Brezhnev thought of the letter is not recorded. It was however reported (by Stephan Hermlin) that it 'went down very badly' with State and Party leaders in East Berlin. Neither of these facts is surprising, for Havemann's appeals had repeatedly touched a very raw nerve in current Soviet and East German policy. It is true that the 'German Question'—the problem of the division of Germany and its possible reunification—had played a not insignificant role in Soviet diplomacy in the early fifties, as repeated notes to the Western powers proposing the creation of a reunited but neutral and demilitarised Germany indicate. But it is equally true that since the 1960s ideas of a reunited Germany have decidedly *not* been any longer a part of the Soviet Union's policies. This is even more true of the GDR, whose leaders, initially wary of a Soviet 'sell-out', have insisted ever more forcefully that there are *two* German states, and that this will remain so: at least, that is, as Honecker recently put it, until the West German working class takes its destiny into its own hands.

In West Germany, the 'German Question' has had a chequered history that has seen it shunted at different moments from one end of the political spectrum to the other. The issue of German reunification, initially a Socialist demand, was, for much of the fifties and sixties, adopted most vociferously by the 'revanchist' Right. During the seventies, in the wake of the 'Ostpolitik', it was largely dropped from the political agenda. But then, at the beginning of the eighties, it started to re-emerge on the Left in the discussions and analyses of the new peace movement, which, especially in West Berlin, began pointing to the inherent links between the cold-war division of Europe and the division of Germany: if something was to be done about the former, so it was argued, then clearly some resolution of the latter problem was not only implied, but might even be a *precondition* of a 'normalisation' of Europe.

Such suggestions—frequently misinterpreted—have been the cause of not a little embarrassment and unease in the West, and have met with some acerbic responses in the West German press. In the East they were absolutely taboo. Havemann's statement that, after the withdrawal of foreign troops, 'How we Germans will then solve our national question will have to be left to us' can only have compounded the iniquity of his letter's earlier reference to American *and Soviet* troops as 'occupation forces' as far as the East German Government was concerned.

Havemann's grand vision of a pacified, reunited Germany in the heart of a nuclear-free Europe is more in keeping with the kinds of debates that are current in the Western peace movements than with the more immediate concerns of the autonomous initiatives in the GDR. It is also, it has been suggested, the vision of a man whose enforced isolation had for too long kept him apart from the experiences, debates, and tactical considerations of grass-roots activists. Certainly, the 'Havemann Initiative' was very quickly adopted by *West* German campaigners, whilst there is little evidence that its discussion of the 'German Question' has struck a particularly resonant chord in the GDR.

Rainer Eppelmann's path to the peace movement followed

61

a more familiar pattern, and the issues he has been concerned with are more in keeping with those of his fellow-Christians in the GDR. A brick-layer by training, he was court-martialled to eight months imprisonment in the mid-sixties for refusing to take the oath on being conscripted; after this he was obliged to serve as a Bausoldat, and then went on to study theology. In 1975 he became a pastor in the Samaritan Church in the East Berlin district of Friedrichshain. There, in 1979, he began organising so-called 'blues masses' (Blues-Messen), folk services involving music, poetry, and discussions aimed especially at young people. Increasingly the 'masses' incorporated discussion and reflection on issues of peace. The State was not amused: the 'Blues-Messen', asserted the Secretary of State for Church Affairs, were 'certainly not a religious service, but a political cabaret' (quoted in *Der Spiegel*, 22 February 1982). Initially, participants came mainly from the local congregation, but more and more young people from outside the area began to attend as word spread throughout the country; today it is not unusual for these 'Blues-Messen' to attract gatherings of five thousand or more.

At the beginning of June 1981 Eppelmann wrote a letter to Erich Honecker (see Documents) in which, in a brisker style and far more forthright terms than the State had come to expect from representatives of the Church, he attacked the many manifestations of militarisation in East German life and the discrimination suffered by those who stood up for peace, and, addressing him in a no-nonsense imperative, requested Honecker to champion publicly the causes of a nuclear-free zone in central Europe, the withdrawal of foreign troops, and step-by-step total disarmament. Receiving no reply, Eppelmann wrote again in early August reminding Honecker of the legal obligation on the authorities to deal with citizens' petitions. Once again no reply was made, and after similarly unsuccessful approaches to the country's leading women's magazine *Für Dich*, to the (East German) Christian Democratic Union's newspaper *Neue Zeit*, and to the chairman of the Writers' Union Hermann Kant, Eppelmann turned to the West German media.

The response this time was more positive: West German

television showed a video-recorded interview with Eppelmann and Havemann in which they spoke about the peace movement in the GDR, their own ideas and objectives, and the problems they both faced in getting these issues discussed. It was an interview that again made clear that the two men approached their common concern from markedly different perspectives. Havemann once more spoke at length of the 'German Question', insisting that he did not envisage a re-united Germany taking the political form of the present-day Federal Republic, but nor did he want it to be like the present GDR with its 'Repressed people. . . . The complete lack of individual freedom in the face of State despotism' (quoted in Ehring and Dallwitz, 224). Again, he asserted his conviction that the GDR was, -in spite of everything, 'the better Germany', but then moved even deeper into the realm of forbidden speculation with the suggestion that he would in fact be willing to sacrifice an awful lot as the price for a re-united Germany:

> If first a kind of multi-party bourgeois democracy like Weimar were to develop. I really don't think it's likely. But I'd even be ready to accept that as the price. It would help get us moving in the right direction.
>
> (Quoted in Ehring and Dallwitz, 225)

Eppelman at this point intervened to say that this was really too complicated a question to go into here and now: it was clear that such visions were not an inherent part of his own more pragmatic thinking, and that he felt some unease at Havemann's wilder speculations.

The 'Berlin Appeal' (see Documents) was formulated by Eppelmann and Havemann early in 1982 and was launched on 25 January. Its title suggests an attempt to respond in kind to the West German 'Krefeld Appeal', which had by then collected some three million signatures. But whereas the 'Krefelder Appell' is a one-issue appeal, demanding the cancellation of the NATO decision to install Cruise and Pershing II missiles in West Germany, the 'Berliner Appell' covers the whole spectrum of East German peace movement concerns—and more besides. Outwardly it bears the stamp of

Eppelmann more than that of Havemann: both its subtitle, 'Make Peace without Weapons'—the motto of the first 'Friedensdekade'—and its quotation from the Sermon on the Mount give it a Christian rather than a Marxist air. Only its introductory points bear unambiguous signs of Havemann's concerns—even down to the contentious reference to the 'occupation forces' still maintained by the wartime allies in their two halves of Germany in point three. The remaining issues, apart from the now much more explicit plea for freedom of expression, were ones that Eppelmann had already broached in his letter to Honecker: by now familiar concerns of the Church such as war toys, 'defence studies', community peace service, the militarisation of public life, and civil defence (here more acerbically referred to as 'so-called' civil defence).

Its comprehensiveness, its forthrightness, its references to the tabooed 'German Question', and—perhaps more than anything—the fact that it was openly canvassing public support, meant that the 'Berlin Appeal' was not only a summation of the concerns of the autonomous peace movement, but also a decidedly dangerous document as far as the authorities were concerned. On 9 February 1982 Eppelmann was arrested, though not before Honecker had taken the unprecedented step of sending a personal telegram to the various ministries 'to put comrades in the picture before they learn what is happening via the Western mass media' (Ehring and Dallwitz, 226). In fact the Western mass media were unable to keep up with events: Eppelmann was released unconditionally twenty-four hours after his arrest, and the State Prosecutor, pressed by the Church, abandoned the judicial inquiry into Eppelmann's activities that had just been initiated. The seventy-three initial signatories too were all summoned to an interview by the State Security Police, where they were asked to withdraw their signatures. None did so; they too were then released.

The State—alarmed at the prospect of an oppositional Marxist-Protestant alliance—was clearly jittery, caught between an instinctive fear of 'subversion', and the desire not to tarnish its image abroad, nor—the speeches of the Berlin Writers' Gathering still fresh in its ears—to lose what credibility it enjoyed with the peace movement at home. One thing was obvious: the only way the Appeal could hope to gain substantial overt support would be if it was adopted by the Churches. Very firm State pressure was now applied behind the scenes on the leadership of Eppelmann's diocese, the Berlin-Brandenburg district; their attention was drawn in particular to paragraphs 106 and 107 of the Penal Code, which deal with offences against the State and provide for penalties of up to twelve years imprisonment for 'incitement to subversion' and 'formation of subversive groupings'. The Church, it was made clear, should not only distance itself from the Appeal, but should also distribute a circular advising against the collection of signatures.

On 13 February 1982 the Berlin Brandenburg Church published its official response to the 'Berlin Appeal' and the State's reaction. 'The Appeal', it stated,

> sets out to express the disquiet and concern for peace that today have gripped above all so many young people. It is also an expression of impatience at the fact that the negotiations of politicians about détente and disarmament might drag on until it is too late. We share this concern and this impatience. They are realities that must be voiced . . .
>
> The Appeal raises a number of questions that have their place in discussions about the Christian responsibility for peace. All the synods of the Federation of Churches have taken up stands on a number of these questions. Many things said in the Appeal belong in these discussions.

But then came the caveats and warnings:

> More precisely than has been done in the Appeal, the reality of the political and military constellation must be borne in mind. The Appeal also paints a distorted picture of those who bear political responsibility. It makes insinuations that have no place in the discipleship of Jesus Christ.
>
> The Church leadership advises emphatically against participation in the collection of signatures, because in that way misunderstandings and risks could arise that would be prejudicial to the necessary objective discussion.
>
> (Quoted in Büscher et al., 283f.)

65

Denied the support of the Church, and faced with the open hostility of the State, the only remaining possibility for the survival of the 'Berlin Appeal' lay in publicity in the West. It was with this in mind that Robert Havemann wrote what was to be his last open letter, on 25 March 1982, to the Western peace movements asking for their support. The cause of the 'Berlin Appeal' was then adopted and widely publicised in West Germany by various sympathetic groupings in the peace movement there, who recognised not only a moral obligation to help their East German friends, but also the opportunity to show the world that there *were* autonomous peace initiatives in Eastern Europe: to offer at least the beginnings of an answer to the banner trailed by a light aircraft above their massive Bonn demonstration, a banner that asked 'Who's demonstrating in Moscow?'.

There was, of course, also a danger in permitting the Appeal to be too enthusiastically embraced in West Germany. It was a danger that the State Security Police had forcefully drawn to the attention of Eppelmann and the other signatories by showing them the headline in a West Berlin paper that read ' "Russians Out" Call by E. Berlin Pastor'. Misuse of the Appeal for anti-Soviet propaganda by the right-wing press could do more harm than good. The 'Berlin Appeal' in any case was *not* an all-German initiative like the Havemann letter to Brezhnev. It was addressed by East Germans to their own government. Support in the West could only take the form of expressions of solidarity with signatories in the GDR, rather than the addition of further signatures to the Appeal itself.

It was in this spirit that the cause of the Appeal was taken up in Britain by END. A translation was printed and signatures were canvassed. The response was heartening: within months nearly 500 people had paid £5 to have their signatures added to the declaration of support. They included many wellknown names from politics, the arts, the sciences, the academic world, and the peace movement generally. That many also came from the left of the political spectrum emphasised that this was no piece of 'anti-Socialist provocation'. The list also included the names of over a hundred organisations that had pledged their support—trade unions and local peace groups figuring prominently among them.

Meanwhile back in the GDR the collection of signatures, despite the obstacles, proceeds in church circles, in people's homes, and at workplaces too. Quite soon over two thousand had been collected. One can assume that that figure has now been multiplied but the true total will never be known: the circulation of the Appeal is, of necessity, decentralised, and the collation of overall totals a virtual impossibility. And now the death of Robert Havemann has left Rainer Eppelmann as the somewhat bemused figurehead *malgré soi* of what the Church at least perceives as the radical wing of the autonomous peace movement. 'All I did was write a letter to Honecker,' he remarks.

The Dresden 'Peace Forum' and 'Swords into Ploughshares'

Little more than two weeks after the launching of the 'Berlin Appeal' the attention of the Western media was drawn to an event in Dresden that was widely interpreted as the clearest evidence yet for the existence of an 'independent peace movement' in the GDR. Already before Christmas 1981 an initiative had been set in motion by small groups of Christians, acting independently of the Church, to commemorate February 13, the thirty-seventh anniversary of the destruction of Dresden by British and American bombers, with a demonstration for peace beside the ruins of the Church of Our Lady. Leaflets to this effect were circulated, and the news spread quickly by word of mouth. The Church authorities were alarmed at the potential for confrontation with the State that such an action would involve, and decided to make the gathering 'legitimate' by organising a 'Peace Forum' in the Church of the Cross that would bring the demonstrators in off the street.

The Dresden 'Peace Forum' was attended by some five thousand young people who had come, despite some official harassment, from all over the Republic. The evening began with a short theatrical sketch, in which a clock with its hands at five to twelve (an echo of Eppelmann's letter to Honecker) was placed next to a flash of lightning—the symbol for 'high voltage'—and the Christian symbol of the cross. A short address by the local Youth Pastor, Harald Bretschneider, and a longer one by the Bishop of Saxony, Johannes Hempel, were then followed by a lengthy discussion, which took the form of a question-and-answer session between the excitable and attentive audience and representatives of the Church: Bretschneider, Hempel, Church President Kurt Domsch, and Joachim Garstecki of the Theological Studies Division in East Berlin.

The position of the Church on issues of peace was now familiar enough: the Church representatives showed a sensitive appreciation of their audience's concerns and interests, but what was most interesting was not so much what they *said* as how the assembled young people *reacted* to what they said. Harald Bretschneider's speech was received with much applause: it was an outspoken address, drawing attention to the areas in which Church and State did not see eye to eye. Two sentences went down particularly well:

> In our television news we see lengthy reports of West European peace movements; and there are many young people who ask why it is so difficult to do such things here. People want to know why in this country, where there is after all so much talk of peace, wearing the 'Swords into Ploughshares' badge, for instance, can lead to so many difficulties.
>
> (Quoted in Büscher et al., 268)

Bishop Hempel's address was also well received, gaining applause, significantly, for the remark that he had 'learnt, in conversation with people like you, of your age, that you are not opposing our Government when you proclaim your initiative' (ibid., 266).

The discussion, however, went at times less smoothly. Most of the Church representatives' remarks were again received with acclamation, but the audience was clearly uneasy on a couple of points: one concerned the problems encountered by people wearing the 'Swords into Plough-shares' badge in public, the other concerned the 'Berlin Appeal'. It was clear that the audience had *heard* of the

68

Appeal, but many had not seen it: they wanted to know more about it, and were decidedly unhappy with the Church's response.

> *Chair:* Some questions have been passed up concerning the 'Berlin Appeal' [applause], for example who originated it, who it is address-ed to, what does it contain, and why doesn't the Regional Church give the 'Berlin Appeal' unconditional support. Why isn't it men-tioned in the Christian Democratic Union's Journal *Union?* (Loud applause, laughter.]
>
> *Church President Domsch:* I can only answer part of the question. The 'Berlin Appeal' was drawn up by the Berlin pastor Eppelmann [applause]. In connection with the 'Berlin Appeal' there is a call to collect signatures. Mr Eppelmann was held for two days 'to enable investigations to proceed' [whistles]. After the Berlin-Brandenburg Church authorities interceded with the Government, he was released again [loud applause]. The investigations were dropped [applause]. The Berlin-Brandenburg Church authorities have discussed the matter in detail and, as far as I know, they have advised against signing the 'Berlin Appeal' on the grounds that both signing and the contents would not help objective discussions about the main-tenance of peace [whistles, boos]. I don't know the wording of the 'Berlin Appeal' [whistles, disturbance]. Please let me finish! The Church authorities here in Saxony haven't looked into these questions yet. But we're sure that Berlin-Brandenburg didn't give that advice without careful thought. So I ask you not to raise the question again [applause, whistles, and boos; heckling].
>
> *Chair:* We've simply got too many questions here. . . [boos, whistles].
>
> *Heckler:* 'Read out the Appeal!' [Applause.]
>
> (Ibid., 276f.)

In fact, for all its agitation, the audience was in too good-natured a frame of mind to press the point too far, and Bishop Hempel was able to get things moving on to the next issue with his plea:

> You really have got to see that the Church has its limits. We're in no way your masters. We're human beings. You must do what you consider right and responsible.
>
> (Ibid., 277)

—a remark that was again greeted with applause.

The debate concluded by carefully leaving open the question of when they would meet again: it was clear the Church could not commit itself to something that might well grow totally beyond its capacity—beyond both the physical and political 'space' that it could offer to such initiatives. As the forum broke up, over a thousand of the participants processed to the Frauenkirche, where, bearing lighted candles, they held a silent vigil. Having left the confines of the church they were now, strictly speaking, breaking the law. The large contingent of police on hand did not, however, interfere.

Many of the participants at the Dresden gathering were wearing an emblem—typically in the form of a fabric badge sewn to their sleeves—that from now on was to be seen, in the West at least, as *the* symbol of the autonomous peace movement in the GDR. Circular in form, it contains in its centre the schematic representation of a man beating a sword into a hammer, and around the edge the words 'Schwerter zu Pflugscharen'. The quotation, as is also indicated in small letters on the badge, is derived from the fourth chapter of the Old Testament Book of Micah (it is also in Isaiah, Chapter Two): 'And they shall beat their swords into ploughshares, and their spears into pruning-hooks: nation shall not lift up a sword against nation, neither shall they learn war any more.' The image of the man represents a piece of sculpture by Evgeny Vuchetich which the Soviet Union presented in 1961 to the United Nations: it stands outside the UN Building in New York.

The 'Swords into Ploughshares' emblem was originally designed for the Churches' first Peace Week in the autumn of 1980. Produced by the Churches in the form of a fabric book-marker, it initially attracted little attention. For the following year's Peace Week, the bookmarkers were again printed, and so were sew-on badges of the emblem. This time they were much more popular. Quickly adopted by numerous young people as a token of their concern for the cause of peace, the book-markers and badges were sewn onto parkas, shirts, and jackets, as well as onto hats and bags. The representation of a Soviet statue could, it seemed, hardly be objected to by the East German authorities, and in any case both it and the slogan 'We will forge swords into plough-shares' had long been contained in the official manual of the 'Jugendweihe'—the secular initiation ritual that the State had introduced in 1955 as a substitute for religious confirmation, and which virtually all fourteen-year-olds now participate in. Even the leading philosophical journal in the GDR was to write in its January 1982 number about the 'Swords into Ploughshares' passage in Micah and Isaiah:

> What Marxist would want to maintain that religious belief in this form was reactionary and—although as yet devoid of a scientifically based awareness—irreconcilable with a scientific approach? This humanist religious belief, as the ideology of progressive classes, to a certain degree anticipates the scientific insight into a classless society in which there are no more wars.
> (*Deutsche Zeitschrift für Philosophie,* quoted in Büscher et al., 17f.)

Nonetheless, the rapidly-spreading badges were causing alarm in State circles: they were perceived as evidence of something that was threatening to get out of hand. Increasingly there were reports of young people being ordered by police to remove their badges, or having them removed if they protested. In many schools and colleges the badges were simply banned, and it even became difficult to be allowed to travel on trains if wearing one. Even a minibus belonging to a pastor was confiscated by the authorities, only to be returned with its stickers removed. Such actions were without clear legal basis, and seemed to be carried out in an unusually haphazard, arbitrary, and uncoordinated fashion. Thus, although the Church representatives reported to the Dresden 'Peace Forum' that they had been able to intervene successfully where difficulties had arisen, and had even received assurances that there would be no more inter-ference with badge-wearers, this did not seem to satisfy many of the young people in the audience, whose own experience did not bear out this optimistic assessment of what was going on.

The 'Peace Forum' seems to have galvanised the authorities into a much more determined campaign against the 'Swords into Ploughshares' emblem. Assurances given earlier to the

Churches that the badges could be worn with impunity were not expressly withdrawn. The State radio declared that those who wore the badge were 'blind, deaf, and hypocritical', whilst the newspaper of the Free German Youth said that the goal of creating peace without weapons was 'in view of the aggressive intentions of imperialism a suicidal illusion' (quoted in Ehring and Dallwitz, 63). Similar sentiments were voiced widely in official quarters, though few went quite as far as the Mayor of the East Berlin borough of Weissensee, who proclaimed to an audience of Church ministers that 'those who wear the "Swords into Ploughshares" emblem will tomorrow be waving the West German flag, and the next day the swastika'—an observation that seems to have gone down rather badly with his listeners, as they all got up and left. (Reported by Jürgen Fuchs in his address to the Bonn peace rally of 10 June 1982.)

There now began a barrage of State counter-slogans, initiated by the Minister of Defence, who made a point of telling the assembled deputies in the People's Chamber that Socialism and peace needed 'our ploughshares *and* our swords'. Another slogan emerged at a 'Writers for Peace' event in East Berlin early in 1982, where the audience were intrigued to find the readings opened by a hitherto unknown young poet by the name of Henry-Martin Klemt. Dressed in army uniform, he dismissed the 'beautiful utopia' of 'Swords into Ploughshares': 'If we forge our swords into ploughshares,' his poem ran, 'they will slaughter us like animals.' At the Whitsun demonstration of the Free German Youth placards appeared bearing the words: 'Swords and Ploughshares, otherwise they'll slaughter us like animals!'

Young people who persisted in wearing the original emblem now found themselves in greater difficulties than ever, confronted with sanctions that included the wrecking of career prospects through expulsions from, or non-admittance to, schools, colleges, and apprenticeships. To give the State's campaign a legal foundation, recourse was not only taken to Paragraph 106 of the Penal Code, which forbids 'subversive symbols', but also to an adjustment to the Decree on Printed Matter: in the GDR all printed material requires a licence, and with the fabric bookmarkers clearly

72

in mind, the Decree was hastily revised to extend this provision to what was cryptically described as 'surface embellishment on textiles'.

The Church's response was on the one hand indignation and concern, but on the other hand there was also resignation in the face of the State's clear determination to keep the use of the emblem under control. Messages read out in the churches in late March and early April talked of discussions that had been held with the Secretary of State for Church affairs, Klaus Gysi, in which he had said:

> Because they have been misused, these badges must not be worn any more in schools or in public . . . they had now become the symbol of an independent peace movement; such a movement could not be tolerated. It was prejudicial to activities by the State and society for the preservation of peace; this made it clear that peace was not the real aim at all.
>
> In another discussion it was even maintained that wearing the badges was a way of expressing disregard for the law and was an incitement to disregard for the law.
>
> (Quoted in Büscher et al., 290)

Another message to congregations explained more fully what the alleged 'misuse' of the badge involved: 'It had been misused to evince a hostile attitude towards the State and participation in an illegal political movement.' In view of all this, the message went on, the Church was now not in a position to protect those who still wore the badges:

> It is not our task as a Church to tell young people what to do in this situation. But we must draw your attention to the threatened consequences, and state clearly that we are no longer able to protect those who wear the badges against them.
>
> (Ibid., 293f.)

In the early summer of 1982 the State changed its tack yet again, and for a while it once more became possible to wear the badges with relative impunity. This approach, however, was in its turn soon abandoned, and by late summer not only had the old forms of intimidation been brought back, but the

Churches began getting reports of a new measure: some young people were having their identity papers withdrawn and replaced with the so-called 'PM12' card, a document that had previously been issued to people who had served a prison sentence or been caught trying to leave the country illegally. Bearers of the 'PM12' are regarded as 'unreliable elements' and may not travel abroad.

Despite such official efforts to suppress the 'Swords into Ploughshares' emblem, it remained for many the distinctive symbol of the GDR's autonomous peace movement. Still widely displayed at gatherings on Church property, it was however henceforth worn with great circumspection elsewhere. Some young people resorted to the expedient of wearing blank patches on their shoulders: so far this has not been banned. Nor, it seems, has the wearing of Soviet postage stamps depicting the Vuchetich sculpture. Indeed, the Soviet Union, which raised no objections to the display of the emblem during the Scandinavian Women's March in July 1982, expressed in June of that year what was widely interpreted as a rebuke to the GDR authorities in the form of a commentary on Radio Moscow. In it, their German specialist Valentin Sacharov discussed the significance of the statue—which he described as 'one of the most outstanding works of Soviet art'—outside the UN Building:

> The Soviet Union, its new, Socialist society, sees reflected in the 'Swords into Ploughshares' sculpture the aims and objectives of its own foreign policy. We believe that the present situation demands of all peoples that they turn swords into ploughshares.
> (Quoted in *Lutherische Welt-Informationen,* 1 July 1982, 16)

Hopes that the Church would take a firm stand on the issue were disappointed when the official Report of the Church Leadership was presented to the annual Synod of the Federation of Evangelical Churches, held in Halle from 24 to 28 September. The Report announced that the emblem would be retained, but, 'for the sake of peace', no longer produced as a badge; it expressed thanks to those young people 'who have borne the symbol as a token of peace and did not allow themselves to become embittered by the

74

measures taken against them', but stressed that it was more appropriate now through words and deeds in the coming Peace Week to counter fears that the symbol was being misused as the badge of an 'organised movement' (*Frankfurter Rundschau,* 18 October 1982). The announcement was not well received by many of those present at the Synod, who felt, in the words of a youth delegate from Dresden, that the trust of young people would be disappointed 'if the Church pays more attention to the worries of the State than to the commitment to peace of young Christians'.

'Swords into Ploughshares' thus remained the motto of the 1982 Peace Week, but this time without the familiar badges. Instead, posters were printed in which both the sculpture and the words appeared, but now separately and in a different layout: the quotation from Micah is there in full, but—in what many gleefully identified as a sly allusion to the ever-busy scissors of the State Security Police—in a format that looks like a clumsy cut-out, retrieved from the wastepaper basket, and resolutely pasted down again.

5

CONCLUSIONS

In the past year or so, official pronouncements have taken increasingly to stressing the *breadth* of the peace movement in the GDR. There is indeed a breadth of approaches and ideas there that is all too often overlooked in the West. But there is also no doubt that the authorities have other reasons than a mere concern for accuracy when they talk of the peace movement in this way. The epithet 'broad', or synonyms such as 'all-embracing' or 'unified', are now almost obligatory accompaniments to the term 'peace movement' when it is used by official spokesmen. Thus, Werner Rümpel, addressing a gathering of the GDR Peace Council, of which he is the General Secretary, said in June 1982.

> In our unified peace movement there is a place for everyone, room for a broad dialogue and action for peace. We shall carry on in the future too the cooperation based on trust and equality that has proven itself over thirty years.
>
> (Quoted in *Neues Deutschland*, 23 June 1982)

It is, in official eyes, a peace movement that is so broad that it includes everyone in the country, which even means that invocations to work harder and produce more—since such zeal will only strengthen the country—are officially construed as active contributions to the cause of peace. Almost any activity in the GDR, be it soldiering, producing, studying, building, farming, or teaching, is liable to be encouraged on its way with the ubiquitous slogan 'Mit unserer Tat für unseren sozialistischen Friedensstaat!'– 'With our Deed for our Socialist Peace State'. As the writer Jan Koplowitz explained in the popular magazine *NBI*:

> It is grotesque to exhort *us* to go out on peace demonstrations and Easter marches when our whole Republic, its citizens, our economy,

76

science and culture, the workers and farmers are one great peace demonstration.

(Quoted in *Die Zeit,* 28 May 1982)

What has been increasingly evident over the past year or so is that the authorities have been concerned to *embrace* grass-roots initiatives as far as possible, and to avoid criminalising them. The concern of the autonomous peace movement has been steadily but firmly to widen that embrace, to keep open and expand the space for dialogue and the breadth of the argument. And the role of the Church in all of this has been the infinitely delicate one of mediator between State and grass roots. Making use of its unique constitutional position, it has sought to protect those whose engagement for peace has led to difficulties with the authorities, to defuse awkward situations, to channel dangerously exposed energies, ideas, and activities into the relative safety of its own 'space'.

Mediators can never satisfy everyone. Rainer Eppelmann gave vent to a not uncommon frustration when he wrote, in the West German magazine *stern* in the autumn of 1981, of the 'disastrous pussy-footing mentality' of the East German churches in their dealings with the State, claiming it had 'reached the dimensions of a perversion' that was undermining the very being of Christianity in the GDR; it was, he said, 'too high a price to pay for the life of the Church'—a sentiment echoed, by more delegates than the Church would have liked, at the 1982 Synod. Klaus Gysi, the Secretary of State for Church Affairs, has—not surprisingly—a different impression of things: 'I can't avoid thinking,' he told leading clerics, 'that you're letting a handful of people terrorise you'.

The attempt of the State to keep the peace movement 'broad', and the determination of the grass roots to make it even broader, have led to some intriguing semantic acrobatics around the word 'independent'—or rather around a number of German words that, confusingly, the standard dictionaries all translate into English as 'independent'. The words in question are, on the one hand, *'unabhängig'*, and, on the other hand, *'selbständig'* and the very similar *'eigenständig'*. The subtle but crucial distinction was made by the leading

Politbüro ideologist Hermann Axen in his closing address to the plenary session of the GDR Peace Council on 16 July 1982:

> The peace movement that is led by the Peace Council of the GDR is a *selbständig* social force. The peace movement must be *selbständig* but it can never be *unabhängig* from the peace state.
>
> (Quoted in *Neues Deutschland*, 17/18 July 1982)

The point was taken by the Chairman of the Federation of Churches, Bishop Werner Krusche, who, in his greetings to Erich Honecker on the occasion of the latter's seventieth birthday, reminded the Party leader that the Church had the right to make 'an *eigenständig* contribution' to the cause of peace in the GDR (*Der Spiegel*, 20 September 1982).

Anyone attempting to decipher these cryptic pronouncements with the aid of a German dictionary gains little enlightenment: the standard definition for 'unabhängig' is 'selbständig', whilst that for 'selbständig' is 'unabhängig'; and the definition for Krusche's term 'eigenständig' is also 'selbständig'. Only etymology can point to a way out: 'unabhängig' means 'not dependent'—in other words quite literally 'in-dependent'. Both 'selbständig' and 'eigenständig' on the other hand are based on the image of 'standing' rather than 'hanging', and imply 'standing on one's own two feet': the one term refers implicitly to links with what is going on *above*, the others to things happening *below*. The point, then, that Axen was making seems to be that the peace movement will always be ultimately answerable to something *above* it—the State, or the Party—but will nonetheless have its feet—or its roots—solidly planted in society at large: the input will come from below, the accountability will be to above.

Such contortions would be laughable were they not so vitally significant. They are part of the earnest game of role-definition and of the marking-out of territory that the State, the Churches, and the autonomous peace initiatives are obliged to play with one another. It is a process that manifests itself most publicly in the battle of the slogans: of 'Swords into Ploughshares' versus 'Swords *and* Ploughshares',

78

of 'Make Peace Without Weapons' ('Frieden schaffen ohne Waffen') versus 'Make Peace against NATO Weapons' ('Gegen NATO-Waffen Frieden schaffen') and 'Peace Must be Defended—Peace Must be Armed'—this latter recently brought back into service after first having seen the light of day with the introduction of conscription in 1961.

Western observers of such goings-on can easily fall into a number of traps. Attempts to assess the nature and implications of peace initiatives in countries such as the GDR are bedevilled by problems of *perspective* and the lack of a due sense of *proportion*. To misunderstand such initiatives is dangerous—especially if it leads to damaging blunders on the part of those who are 'only trying to help'.

At the root of these difficulties is a tendency to leap all too readily to conclusions about the East European movements by bringing inappropriate criteria to bear: the habit of looking at facts rather than factors, of imposing a West European context on East European events. This is an error of perspective that can lead all too easily to seeing the 'autonomous' peace movement in the GDR as somehow irremediably *opposed* to the State and its policies. This is not the case. Time and again the Churches, and the groupings and individuals working within and around them, have acknowledged the achievements and morality of Socialism, they have affirmed the State's peace initiatives, and those of the Soviet Union. Time and again they have criticised American armament policies, in full unanimity with the criticisms voiced by their own government. And when they have not done so it has been because their resolute opposition to such matters as the threatened deployment of Cruise and Pershing II is already well-known: a starting-point for discussion that hardly needs reiterating. The autonomous peace movement in the GDR is neither 'anti-Socialist' nor 'anti-Soviet': to talk of its supporters as 'dissidents' is to misconstrue—innocently or otherwise—the whole constellation of events and attitudes.

The truth is that opinion in the GDR is not divided into two distinct and hostile camps: it is rather a matter of a continuum, a spectrum of ideas and attitudes, in which debate is conducted not just between the two ends, but

79

between each and every position along the line (a debate, it might be added, that proceeds with far greater intellectual precision than is all too often the case in the West). Nor is it simply a matter of arguments between 'Christians' and 'Marxists'. There are Christians who give implicit support both to the State's policies and to its philosophy: they are represented in the People's Chamber by the fifty-two deputies of the CDU—a party whose emblem incorporates the words 'Ex oriente pax'. Other Christians may not care so much for the official *philosophy,* but nonetheless go along with the State's foreign policy and all that that implies. More 'radical' Christians, and in particular the new generation of young pastors who are playing such a vital role in the peace movement, and members of the 'Evangelical Student Congregations' in some universities, are often happy to proclaim their support for Socialism, but at the same time do not accept the military implications that the State—and the CDU—would find in this.

And then there is the ever-growing number of young people who find themselves drawn into the peace movement: some are committed Christians, many are probably not; most would probably describe themselves, if pressed, as 'Socialists'. Many will take part in officially sponsored rallies: partly because it is expected of them, but also because they *are* opposed to the NATO weaponry and policies that such events decry. Many will see no contradiction in marching loudly for peace with the FDJ—the Free German Youth—and gathering quietly for peace in a local church. One has only to look at the way FDJ shirts so often go with jeans, parkas, and long hair to appreciate the mingling of the cultures and attitudes. (The authorities even tried to make the most of this by getting a team of fashion designers to give the Whitsun '82 rallies a peacenik look, right down to white head-bands for the FDJ contingents.)

Difficulties of perspective can also lead to a false sense of proportion. We are trained by the media to measure the importance of events—be they strikes, demonstrations, or petitions—by the numbers of participants. Such a yardstick can often be inappropriate in the West; it can be even more misleading if our unfamiliarity with Eastern Europe leads us

80

to underestimate the significance of things going on there because they seem to involve only a small minority of people. This does not mean, on the other hand, that we should allow ourselves to fall into the opposite error of *exaggerating* the importance of particular events: by focusing *our* attention on certain contentious issues, we can equally easily give ourselves the false impression that these are things the average East German is deeply concerned about.

It may well be that the average East German has not even heard of some of these issues, though this is unlikely. The majority of East Germans, via Western television, are more regularly confronted with Western perceptions of what *they* are supposed to be thinking about than any other Eastern Europeans, let alone the people of the Soviet Union. And this leads to one other common error of perception: that of seeing the countries of 'Eastern Europe' as all identical with one another. There are great differences between them in all kinds of respects, and that goes for the preconditions for—and hence the nature of—autonomous peace activity as much as anything.

It is all too easy to fall into a self-congratulatory Western perspective when looking at events in the GDR. Perhaps the most salutary lesson that the peace movement in the GDR can teach us is that relations between the grass roots and the authorities there show remarkable parallels with the experiences of Western movements: they too are confronted with a militaristic ethos, with arguments about 'deterrence', the need to be 'strong', and accusations that they, unwittingly or otherwise, are 'doing the other side's job for them'. The official philosophy of the West that there is a 'global military threat' from the Soviet Union is reflected exactly in that selfsame 'global military threat' that in the East is seen to emanate from the imperialism of the USA. There are differences, major differences, of degree between what autonomous initiatives can do in the East and what they can do in the West, but the problem that confronts them is the same.

With this in mind, one more little incident from 'the heart of the GDR' may be reported. In May 1982 there was a major military parade in Berlin. A small number of people

81

turned out to demonstrate peaceably against it by distributing and displaying the 'Swords into Ploughshares' emblem. Without warning, they were violently attacked by the police, and their leaflets were confiscated. The incident received little coverage in the media. It occurred in West Berlin; the parade was the annual display of strength by the Western garrisons in the city. The police were acting at their request.

THE 'BAUSOLDATEN' DECREE

7 September 1964

(See pp. 28 –32)

Decree of the National Defence Council of the German Democratic Republic on the formation of Construction Units under the Ministry of National Defence

I

(1)   Construction Units are to be formed under the Ministry of National Defence.

(2)   Service in the Construction Units is alternative national service in accordance with Paragraph 25 of the Conscription Law of 24 January 1962. It will be undertaken without arms.

II

(1)   The Construction Units will have the task of performing work in the interests of the German Democratic Republic. In particular this will include:

   a) Helping with road building and other traffic works, and the extension of defensive and other military installations.
   b) Making good damage caused by manoeuvres.
   c) Disaster relief work.

(2)   The Construction Units will operate on the instruction of the Minister of National Defence or his representatives.

III

Members of the Construction Units are subject to the same legal and military provisions as ordinary conscripts and reservists in the National People's Army, unless otherwise stipulated in this Decree.

IV

(1)   Those liable for call-up who reject armed service on the basis of religious views or similar grounds will be conscripted into the Construction Units.

(2)   Members of the Construction Units will have the rank of 'Bausoldat' ('Construction Soldier').

V

(1)   Members of the Construction Units will not make an oath of allegiance as prescribed in the Service Ordinance of 24 January 1962.

(2)   Members of the Construction Units will make a vow (see Appendix).

VI

In addition to enlistment for work in accordance with Paragraph II (1), members of the Construction Units will receive instruction as follows:

    a) Political instruction,
    b) Instruction in legal and military regulations,
    c) Unarmed drill,
    d) Military physical training,
    e) Sapper duties and specialist training,
    f) Civil defence training,
    g) First aid training.

VII

Bausoldaten in the Construction Units will wear a stone-grey buttoned uniform with olive-coloured braidings. As a distinguishing mark they will wear the symbol of a spade on their epaulettes.

VIII

Reservists who have not previously served and who meet the provisions of Paragraph IV (1), and Reservists who have previously served in Construction Units, may in place of Reserve duty, be conscripted into Construction Units for training or exercises.

IX

The superiors of the members of the Construction Units (training personnel) will be experienced soldiers, NCOs, and officers of the National People's Army.

X

In the interest of increased productivity members of the Construction Units may, as a material incentive, be paid supplements over and above normal army pay. The pre-condition for supplementary payments will be work that exceeds the prescribed requirements.

XI

The Minister of National Defence will issue the necessary enactments and military provisions for the enactment of this Decree.

XII

This Decree is effective as of 1 September 1964.

Appendix (to Paragraph V (2) of the above Decree)

VOW

I VOW:
At all times faithfully to serve the German Democratic Republic, my homeland, and to put my efforts into increasing its defensive capabilities.

I VOW:
As a member of the Construction Units, by working well to contribute actively to ensuring that the National People's Army, alongside the Soviet Army and the armies of our Socialist allies, can protect the Socialist state against all enemies and achieve victory.

I VOW:
To be honest, brave, disciplined, and alert, to obey my

superiors unconditionally, to carry out their orders resolutely, and never to divulge military and state secrets.

I VOW:
Conscientiously to acquire the knowledge necessary for carrying out my tasks, to comply with legal and military regulations, and everywhere to preserve the honour of our Republic and of my Unit.

(Source: *Gesetzblatt der Deutschen Demokratischen Republik,* Part I, No. 11 (16 September 1964), 129f. Reproduced in Eisenfeld, 213f.)

THE 'COMMUNITY PEACE SERVICE' INITIATIVE

Dresden, May 1981

(See pp. 32 – 33)

Dear Friends,

We are continuing to look for ways to attain peace. Because of our 'Respect for Life' we must make peace without weapons, and do all we can for life under threat.

We are deeply troubled by the constant growth in armaments in both West and East. We are troubled by the ever-growing weight of the military aspect in our society. Troubled too on the other hand by shortcomings in the social sphere—the problems of the sick, of the physically and mentally handicapped, of old people in homes and nursing homes, of addicts, and of the rehabilitation of ex-prisoners. In these areas there is a recognised shortage of personnel.

This shortage could be partially alleviated by auxiliary staff, who would contribute their goodwill and humanity. The skilled personnel would be able to give their full attention to their proper tasks.

On 25 April and 9 May 1981 we met in Dresden and worked further on the 'Community Peace Service' initiative ('Sozialer Friedensdienst'–'SoFd'), which has been discussed for half a year now. The revised text is given below. Our initiative is intended as a concrete contribution to the practice of peace, and as a way of benefiting those in our society who are in most urgent need of help.

Community Peace Service

We ask the People's Chamber of the GDR to legislate as follows:

1.   As a fully equal alternative to both regular and unarmed military service, a Community Peace Service will be established. Recruitment, selection, and enlistment will accord with

normal draft procedure. The Universal Conscription Law of 24 January 1962 and ensuing provisions are to be amended accordingly.

2. Those performing Community Peace Service will be required to serve for 24 months:
  – as a symbolic 'handicap' attesting to their desire for peace
  – as a disincentive for 'shirkers'.

3. Community Peace Service will enjoy the same rights as military service (e.g. insurance, pay, leave, security of former job).

4. Provision for quartering in hostels may be made to avoid the unfair advantage of living at home.

5. Basic training in first aid and disaster relief will be given.

6. Those performing Community Peace Service will receive regular political instruction, with special emphasis on the safeguarding of peace, disarmament, and non-violent conflict resolution.

7.1 Those performing Community Peace Service will be employed in social priority areas:

  – homes (for children, old people, the sick, and the physically or mentally handicapped)
  – auxiliary service in hospitals
  – social work (among addicts and young people; rehabilitation work)
  – community care
  – consideration should be given to environmental protection work.

7.2 The aims of this plan are:
  – relieving the pressure on skilled personnel to enable them to concentrate on their proper tasks
  – relieving those with family commitments of night and weekend duties.

If you are in sympathy with this initiative, talk about it with your friends. Write to the Synod of the Church in your area before 1 September 1981 (World Peace Day).

It depends on you, and on each and everyone!

(Source: Büscher et al., 169-71; also in Ehring and Dallwitz, 186-7.)

THE 'HAVEMANN INITIATIVE'

20 September 1981

(See pp. 60 – 61)

An Open Letter to the Chairman of the Presidium of the Supreme Soviet of the USSR, Leonid Brezhnev

Dear Mr Leonid Brezhnev,

Filled with anxiety about the future of Europe and world peace, we turn to you in the hope that your planned visit this autumn to the Federal Republic of Germany and your meeting with Chancellor Helmut Schmidt will open up a way out of the present dangerous course of events.

More and more people are afraid that after over thirty years of peace in Europe, our continent is now threatened with total destruction in a nuclear world war. In Western Europe this fear manifests itself in particular in the opposition to new American medium-range missiles, the building of the neutron bomb, and the nuclear weapons stored in Europe. If these weapons are ever used, they will turn Europe into a desert.

It is well known that the advocates of this policy describe this so-called enhancement of the NATO armoury as purely defensive. It is, they say, merely a response to the arming of the Warsaw Pact countries with new medium-range SS-20 missiles, with their similar range, and to the great numerical superiority of the Soviet tank force.

In view of the magnitude of the danger that threatens us, we see little point in asking whether there are any other reasons for this escalation of terror. How can the deployment of the rockets, cruise missiles, and neutron bombs be prevented? How can Europe, where today there is a greater accumulation of nuclear warheads than in any other part of the world, be turned into a nuclear-weapon-free zone?

Although we signatories of this letter have very different ideas about the reasons for these dangerous developments, we would start from the premise that the original aims of both NATO and the Warsaw Pact are not aggressive, and that they are purely defensive in character. Unfortunately however, in the course of the years a terrifying arms race on both sides has led to the fact that today two military machines bristling with weapons stand face to face on the dividing line in Europe. They have at their disposal a destructive capacity sufficient to kill the whole of humanity not just once, but perhaps five or ten times over. The main reason for this arms race is that neither side any longer believes that the other's intentions are purely defensive.

Rather, each side is convinced that a growing threat must be countered with ever renewed efforts in the field of weaponry. The dangers of this are self-evident. In the increasing gravity of military confrontation in Europe the division of Germany plays a crucial role. Originally it seemed that a dangerous aggressor had in this way been rendered permanently powerless, thereby securing peace in Europe. But the result was the exact opposite. For if the nuclear holocaust should some day overtake us, it will result above all from the fact that the confrontation between East and West turned the two German states into bases for deployment and nuclear spearheads directed each against the other. The division of Germany has not brought security: it has instead become the precondition for the most deadly threat that has ever existed in Europe.

Every bomb, every missile, every weapon of any sort that our protectors bring to Germany does not secure peace, but brings us instead closer to destruction. We do not need to arm, but to disarm. We do not need the strength of NATO and the Warsaw Pact, but the continuation of global policies of détente, so that NATO and the Warsaw Pact may one day become superfluous. The security of Europe will not come from weapons of war, but from their abolition.

It is especially vital to withdraw the two parts of Germany from the confrontation between the blocs. It should in this context be remembered that, right through to the 1960s, the Soviet Union made repeated calls for the demilitarisation and neutralisation of the whole of Germany. Thirty-six years after the end of the war it has now become an urgent necessity to conclude the peace treaties, and to withdraw all

90

occupation forces from both parts of Germany. (Naturally the position of West Berlin would have to remain safeguarded.) How we Germans will then solve our national question will have to be left to us, and no-one should find this more frightening than atomic war.

To many Germans this goal appears desirable, but for the time being utopian. They cannot imagine the Soviet Union being prepared to renounce its military presence in the GDR. We believe, however, that this is perfectly possible if at the same time the military presence of the USA in West Germany —and thus in the whole of Europe—is brought to an end. It should equally be stipulated in the peace treaty, and guaranteed by the great powers, that no aggressive military potential shall ever again be created in Germany.

Dear Mr Brezhnev: At what may well be the eleventh hour, we implore you to give these proposals your earnest consideration. We are convinced that no West German government can continue to insist on the installation of the new American nuclear weapons if the government of the Soviet Union declares itself ready to negotiate a proposal such as this for resolving the tensions in Europe, and if moreover it facilitates such negotiations by itself refraining from expanding still further the existing medium-range weaponry directed at Western Europe.

In view of the fact that the Second World War that Germany started brought to your country the loss of 20 million people, and in view of the 5 million dead mourned by our own people, security and the safeguarding of peace must—for our two peoples especially—be the most urgent political priority.

Yours most respectfully,
Robert Havemann

THE 'EPPELMANN LETTER'

June 1981

(See pp. 62 – 63)

Dear Mr Honecker,

It is five minutes to twelve. The suicidal arms race of the past years has made the danger of a nuclear conflict in Europe greater than ever. Vast quantities of raw materials and energy, of money and human ingenuity, of time and labour, are being irresponsibly squandered. Yet if we are to master the problems that confront humankind at the end of our century, we need all the powers at our disposal. As a consequence of this wasteful creation of weaponry and discord, fear, mistrust, hatred, aggression, and resignation have increasingly come to dominate relations between individuals and peoples. Unless all peace-loving people give each other mutual support and encouragement, and urge the rulers of their countries to do all they can for greater trust between individuals and peoples, the danger of the nuclear annihilation of Europe will continue to grow. For this reason, pacifism is today no longer just one possible way of conducting politics, but, in view of the great danger of the total destruction of all life, the sole possibility for political action.

Politicians who include military conflict in their political calculations are planning genocide, and are thus acting neither in the interests of humankind, nor at its behest. As a convinced Christian and pacifist I therefore ask you to contribute, with all the means at your disposal, to preventing the destruction with which Europe is threatened. Give concrete support to the peoples' wish for peace. Give powerful additional arguments to the Western European supporters of wide-scale disarmament. Give the NATO countries' rulers the certainty that you really do want disarmament and peace. Take away the mistrust that exists among the peoples of Western Europe by acting without delay. Help trust to grow between the peoples of Europe. In order to achieve this,

I propose the following confidence-building measures to you: they involve no risk to the security of the GDR, or at most a minimal one that you can easily take account of.

1.   A ban on the production, sale, possession, and import of war toys.
2.   A ban on the glorification of soldierhood in education, schoolbooks, and in work outside the schools.
3.   The abolition of organised visits to barracks by kindergarten groups and school classes.
4.   The abolition of defence studies and pre-military training in schools and vocational courses.
5.   The replacement of the above by Peace and Life Studies, with, for instance, the following contents: possibilities of non-violent conflict resolution; questions of partnership between husband and wife and coexistence within the family; questions of education; study of the laws on environmental protection, and introduction to psychology.
6.   The abolition of the preferential treatment in terms of finance and jobs accorded to school pupils, apprentices, and students who intend to take up a military career.
7.   At the same time as this, the abolition of the discrimination suffered by those pupils, apprentices, and students who do not take up a military career.
8.   Full equality of rights for alternative national service and the abolition of the discrimination suffered by Bausoldaten in their career prospects.
9.   The transformation of alternative national service into a community service independent of the army.
10.   The abolition of the privileges enjoyed by those who have stayed in the army for a lengthy period.
11.   No grandiose military parades, and no military presentations at fêtes and suchlike—e.g. the *Neues Deutschland* Press Festival, the Weissensee Flower Festival.
12.   The abandonment of all military demonstrations on the occasion of national holidays and state visits.
13.   No more discrimination against pupils, apprentices, and students who express pacifist convictions.
14.   Speak up publicly for a nuclear-weapons-free zone in central Europe.

15. Speak up publicly for the removal of all foreign troops from all the countries of Europe.
16. Speak up publicly for the demilitarisation of the two German states.
17. Speak up publicly for gradual total disarmament.

It is five minutes to twelve, therefore we must take a chance, we must create trust, we must give people fresh heart, we must build a lasting peace. Thank you for any help you might be able to give.

Yours sincerely,
Rainer Eppelmann

(Sources: Büscher et al., 178-80; Ehring and Dallwitz, 218-20.)

THE 'BERLIN APPEAL—MAKE PEACE WITHOUT WEAPONS'

25 January 1982

(See pp. 63 –67)

1. There is only one kind of war that could still take place in Europe, nuclear war. The weapons stockpiled in the East and the West will not protect us, but destroy us. We will all be long dead when the soldiers in their tanks and at the missile base, as well as the generals and politicians in their bunkers, on whose protection we have relied, are still living and continuing to destroy whatever remains.

2. If therefore we want to remain alive—away with the weapons! And first of all: away with the nuclear weapons. The whole of Europe must become a nuclear-weapons-free zone. We propose that there should be negotiations between the governments of the two German states about the removal of all nuclear weapons from Germany.

3. Divided Germany has become the deployment area for the two nuclear superpowers. We propose an end to this potentially fatal confrontation. The victors of World War Two must finally conclude peace treaties with both German states, as decided in the Potsdam Agreement of 1945. Thereafter, the former Allies should withdraw their occupation troops from Germany and agree on guarantees of non-intervention in the internal affairs of the two German states.

4. We propose that the great debate about questions of peace be conducted in an atmosphere of tolerance and recognition of the right of free expression, and that every spontaneous public manifestation of the desire for peace should be approved and encouraged. We appeal to the public and our government to discuss and reach decisions on the following questions:

a) Should we not renounce the production, sale, and import of so-called war toys and games?
b) Should we not introduce lessons about problems of peace in our schools in place of 'defence studies'?
c) Should we not allow a community peace service for conscientious objectors instead of the present kind of alternative to military service?
d) Should we not renounce all demonstrations of military strength in public and instead use our national celebrations for declaring the people's desire for peace?
e) Should we not renounce so-called civil-defence exercises? Since there is no possibility of meaningful civil defence in a nuclear war, these exercises simply play down the real nature of nuclear war. Is it not really a method of psychological preparation for war?

5. Make peace without weapons—that does not only mean ensuring our own survival. It also means finishing with the senseless waste of labour and of the wealth of our people on the production of arms, and the equipping of gigantic armies of young people, who are thereby removed from productive work. Should we not rather be helping the starving all over the world instead of continuing to prepare our own death?

Blessed are the meek:
for they shall inherit the earth.
(Jesus of Nazareth in the Sermon on the Mount)

The balance of terror has prevented nuclear war up to now only by postponing it until tomorrow. The peoples of the world regard the approach of this gruesome tomorrow with dread. They are searching for new ways to improve the foundations of peace. The 'Berlin Appeal' is one expression of this search. Think about it, make proposals to our politicians, and everywhere discuss the question: What will bring about peace; what will bring about war?

Affirm your support for the 'Berlin Appeal' by signing below.

Berlin, 25 January 1982

(Source: Büscher et al., 242-4; also in Ehring and Dallwitz, 227-9.)

THE 'WOMEN'S LETTER'

October 1982

(See p. 33)

To Erich Honecker, Chairman of the Council of State of the GDR:

Dear Mr Chairman,

In this letter we would like to put before you some thoughts about the conscription of women that have been troubling us since the passing of the new Conscription Law of 25 March 1982. We are women with and without children, Catholics, Protestants, and without church affiliations; some of us have experienced a war, others have been spared this dreadful experience. But one thing unites us all, and that is the fact that we are not indifferent, and are not willing to give silent assent to a law that imposes totally new obligations on women, obligations that cannot be reconciled with the way we see ourselves.

— We women want to break the circle of violence and to withdraw from participation in the use of violence as a means of resolving conflicts.

— We women do not see military service for women as an expression of their equal rights, but as a contradiction of their womanhood. We do not see that our equality with men consists in standing alongside *those* men who take up arms, but alongside *those* who, like us, have recognised that the abstract terms 'enemy' and 'opponent' are tantamount to the destruction of human beings—a destruction that we reject.

— We women regard preparedness for military service as a threatening gesture that stands in the way of moral and military disarmament, drowning the voice of human reason in military obedience.

— We women feel we have a special duty to protect life, to support the old, the sick, and the weak. Activity for peace and against war can only take place in the social and educational spheres if we are not to fail the next generation.

97

— We women oppose the idea that one day we are to stand in the ranks of the National People's Army and defend a country that will be uninhabitable, even after a conventional war, which in Europe would probably end in a nuclear catastrophe.

— We women believe that humanity stands today on the edge of an abyss, and that the accumulation of more weapons will lead to an insane catastrophe. This terrible end can perhaps be prevented if all the questions arising from this fact are publicly discussed. According to Article 65, Paragraph 3 of the Constitution of the GDR, drafts of laws of a fundamental nature are supposed to be presented to the people for discussion before they are passed, so that the results of this popular discussion can be evaluated when the final version is formulated. In our opinion, this law is of a fundamental nature because of the topic it deals with, and not least because one half of the GDR's population is *directly* affected.

— We women declare that we are not prepared to be included in general conscription, and we demand a legal guarantee for the option of conscientious objection. The right to refuse military service is necessary because the passing of this law, which imposes on women the obligation to do general military service, represents a restriction on our freedom of conscience.

Since no public discussions on this law have been possible, some of us have requested such discussions by means of petitions; others hope to be able to participate in the ensuing dialogues. Unfortunately these expectations have been disappointed, for no-one has been prepared to begin a dialogue about the questions that are of such acute concern to us.

The speech delivered by Academician Professor Arbatov at the world religious peace congress in Moscow encouraged us once again to address our questions to you. We ask that those responsible for this new Conscription Law also be prepared to engage in open dialogue. You are undoubtedly familiar with this speech, but we would still like to quote a few sentences.

Professor Arbatov deals among other things with the psychological and moral allies of the arms race, and refers to the myth that the accumulation of weapons and military

98

forces would contribute to security.

'All of these myths promote the arms race. Nowadays the attempt is made to wrap them up in complicated ideas and enigmas by using terminology that the lay person cannot understand. I wouldn't be surprised if this is done deliberately in order to keep the "unitiated" and the "man in the street" at bay. It's even said on various occasions that this man shouldn't be allowed too close to questions of nuclear weaponry, or problems of war and peace, because he would only muddle everything up and cause damage. But in my opinion this is the most dangerous and detrimental myth of all! . . . This problem must be solved through everybody's active participation . . . if it's human beings rather than weapons that are to be served.'

We could not have found a better argument for the necessity of our petition.

We ask you to facilitate an open dialogue for us.

(Source: *Der Spiegel,* No. 49, 6 December 1982, p. 117.)

CHRONOLOGY

Any selection of events is bound to be somewhat arbitrary. The following list indicates in sequence some of the events—both within and outside the GDR—that have some bearing on the development and activities of the autonomous peace movement.

1945 May

Capitulation of Nazi Germany; the four wartime Allies take over administration of their respective Zones of Occupation.

1946 21–22 April

In the Soviet Zone the Communist Party (KPD) and the Social Democrat Party (SPD) are merged to form the Socialist Unity Party of Germany (SED), which assumes an increasingly influential role.

1949 4 April

Establishment of NATO.

23 May

British, American, and French Zones of Occupation become the German Federal Republic ('West Germany').

7 October

Soviet Zone of Occupation becomes the German Democratic Republic ('East Germany').

1950 10 May

Establishment in East Berlin of the 'German Committee of Fighters for Peace'—re-named 'Peace Council of the GDR' in 1963.

1955 9 May

West Germany joins NATO.

14 May

Establishment of Warsaw Pact (including GDR).

1956	1 January	Volunteer army established in West Germany.
	3 March	Volunteer army established in GDR.
	21 July	Conscription (with provisions for conscientious objection) intro-. duced in West Germany.
1961	13 August	Erection of Berlin Wall.
1962	24 January	Conscription (with no provisions for conscientious objection) introduced in GDR.
1964	7 September	Provisions for conscientious objection ('Bausoldaten Decree') introduced in GDR.
1969	10 June	Protestant Churches in GDR break formal ties with West German Churches to form the 'Federation of Evangelical Churches in the GDR'.
1971	5 May	Erich Honecker replaces Walter Ulbricht as First Secretary of the SED.
1973	21 June	'Basic Treaty' between West Germany and the GDR—a cornerstone of the 'Ostpolitik' agreements—comes into effect, 'normalising' relations and facilitating contacts between citizens of the two German states.
	1 August	Death of Walter Ulbricht.
1976	29 October	Erich Honecker elected Chairman

		of the Council of State (de facto: head of state).
1978	6 March	Meeting between Protestant Church leadership and State and Party leaders.
	September	Introduction of 'Defence Studies' into school syllabus.
1979	Autumn	USSR begins withdrawal of 20,000 troops and 1,000 tanks from GDR.
	12 December	NATO Cruise and Pershing II decision.
1980	9–19 November	First all-German Church 'Peace Week'.
	15–16 November	Launch of 'Krefeld Appeal' provides rallying-point for West German peace movement.
1981	May	'Community Peace Service' initiative.
	June	'Eppelmann Letter' to Erich Honecker.
	20 June	First big peace movement rally of the 1980s in West Germany: 80,000 demonstrate at the Protestant Church Assembly in Hamburg.
	20 September	'Havemann Initiative' to Leonid Brezhnev.
	10 October	Second big rally in West Germany: 300,000 demonstrate in Bonn.
	8–18 November	Second all-German Church 'Peace Week'.

	13–14 December	Berlin Writers' Gathering.
1982	25 January	'Berlin Appeal' appears.
	9 February	Rainer Eppelmann arrested.
	11 February	Rainer Eppelmann released.
	13 February	Dresden 'Peace Forum'.
	25 March	New Conscription Law—including provisions for call-up of women in times of crisis.
	9 April	Death of Robert Havemann.
	10 June	Third big rally in West Germany: 400,000 demonstrate in Bonn.
	October	'Women's Letter' to Erich Honecker.
	7–17 November	Third all-German Church 'Peace Week'.
	24 December	Silent demonstration in Jena leads to arrests.
1983	2 January	Catholic bishops issue first major statement on peace.
	February	Release of the Jena detainees.

BIBLIOGRAPHY

There is very little material available in English: the only significant survey so far is the English version of the Dutch Inter-Church Peace Council's pamphlet 'Peace Activities in the GDR' (available from: IKV, Postbus 18747, 2502 ES 's-Gravenhage, Netherlands).

For general information on the GDR, the following two books are invaluable:

Peter Christian Ludz (ed.), *DDR Handbuch,* Verlag Wissenschaft und Politik, Cologne 1979 (an encyclopaedic West German handbook).

Kleines Politisches Wörterbuch, Dietz Verlag, East Berlin, 1978 (an authoritative East German dictionary of politics).

The various versions of the GDR's Constitutions are contained in:

Rudolf Schuster (ed.), *Deutsche Verfassungen,* Wilhelm Goldmann Verlag, Munich 1978.

Two important West German books on the peace movement in the GDR have recently appeared:

Wolfgang Büscher/Peter Wensierski/Klaus Wolschner/Reinhard Henkys, *Friedensbewegung in der DDR. Texte 1978–1982,* Scandica-Verlag, Hattingen 1982 (an anthology of documents, especially from Church sources, with introduction and commentary).

Klaus Ehring/Martin Dallwitz, *Schwerter zu Pflugscharen. Friedensbewegung in der DDR,* Rowohlt Taschenbuch Verlag, Reinbek 1982 (surveys the issues and events involving the autonomous peace movement; also contains several documents).

A briefer account is contained in Hans-H. Hücking's article 'Die Friedensbewegung in der DDR', on pp. 258–83 of: of:

Reiner Steinweg (ed.), *Die neue Friedensbewegung. Analysen aus der Friedensforschung,* Suhrkamp Verlag, Frankfurt am Main 1982.

A slightly older, thoroughly researched and well documented history of conscientious objection in the GDR by a former Bausoldat now living in the West is:

Bernd Eisenfeld, *Kriegsdienstverweigerung in der DDR— ein Friedensdienst? Genesis, Befragung, Analyse, Dokumente,* Haag und Herchen Verlag, Frankfurt am Main 1978.

The proceedings of the Berlin Writers' Gathering are contained in full in:

Berliner Begegnung zur Friedensförderung. Protokolle des Schriftstellertreffens am 13./14. Dezember 1981, Hermann Luchterhand Verlag, Darmstadt and Neuwied 1982.

Extracts from the Gathering, together with excerpts from the proceedings of the subsequent writers' gatherings in The Hague and Cologne are assembled in:

Bernt Engelmann/Gerd E. Hoffman/Angelika Mechtel/ Hans v.d. Waarsenburg, *'Es geht, es geht...' Zeitgenössische Schriftsteller und ihr Beitrag zum Frieden— Grenzen und Möglichkeiten,* Wilhelm Goldmann Verlag, Munich 1982.

105

The Friedrich-Ebert-Stiftung (Godesberger Allee 149, 5300 Bonn 2) in its series 'Die DDR: Realitäten—Argumente' has produced a booklet on the peace movement in the GDR, as well as one on militarisation in daily life, and one on the status of the Church:

Die Friedensbewegung in der DDR (1982).
Wehrpropaganda und Wehrerziehung in der DDR (1982).
Kirche und Staat in der DDR und in der Bundesrepublik (1981).

POSTSCRIPT

MARCH 1983

Developments in the first couple of months of 1983 indicate a growing unease on the part of the State at the spread of autonomous peace initiatives in the GDR—an unease compounded with alarm at evidence of a marked increase in the number of applications for Bausoldat status. But there are also signs that the authorities are still responsive to the negative consequences of the criminalisation of grass-roots activities.

At the beginning of the year, the Catholic Church in the GDR broke with its traditional reticence, and addressed itself to the problems of peace in terms akin to those already commonplace among Protestants. At the same time, news began reaching the West of a silent demonstration in Jena on Christmas Eve. The heavy-handed official response to both of these events suggested a hardening of the State's attitude to autonomous and Church-based initiatives; other reports from the GDR—including indications that in some cases applicants for Bausoldat status are being turned down, and persistent applicants arrested—backed up this impression; they also suggest a certain radicalisation among sections of the peace movement that manifests itself in impatience and a growing wariness on the part of some young people towards not only the State, but also the Church—at least in its institutional guise.

More recent reports indicate, however, that the State may have had second thoughts about the tougher new approach. The 1983 commemoration of the destruction of Dresden, for example—which has now also become the anniversary of the 1982 'Peace Forum'—passed off quietly. Alongside the large official rally, the Church carefully dispersed its own more low-key events over a number of localities: large numbers of young people still came to the four different discussions that had been arranged, and some 200 of them again went afterwards to stand—without harassment—before the ruins of the Frauenkirche.

The significant new forthrightness of the Catholic Church emerged in a pastoral letter of the GDR's ten bishops, read out to congregations on 2 January. The letter spoke critically of the growing role of military activities in education, of the compulsive perpetual reinforcement of 'deterrence', of the philosophy of the 'just war'; it expressed 'respect' towards conscientious objectors, and addressed itself favourably to the 'Community Peace Service' ideal. The State's public response was minimal, but frosty. The letter itself was not reported in the East German media, but on 7 January an editorial appeared in *Neues Deutschland* ostensibly attacking the hypocrisy of those media in the Federal Republic that portrayed recent proposals to introduce 'defence studies' in *West* German schools as a 'contribution to peace', whilst they at the same time criticised the *genuine* contribution to peace represented by 'defence studies' in schools in the GDR. Then, in a cryptic closing sentence, came a thinly-veiled allusion to the bishops' letter:

> The fact that they [the West German media] have recently received the blessing of certain dignitaries in the GDR, who are controlled from Rome, doesn't make things any better; it makes one wonder— not only about certain mass media in the Federal Republic, but also about certain dignitaries who are citizens of the GDR.

Regular readers of *Neues Deutschland* will have noted that a couple of numbers later the Party organ devoted a whole page to an enthusiastic account of the peace proposals of Catholic bishops in the USA.

The events that occurred in the south-western university town of Jena on Christmas Eve 1982 were a further indication of the discontent among young people that has been particularly evident in that part of the GDR for some time; more importantly, they were also evidence of the State's increasing concern that this discontent might develop and spread into a more widescale disaffection. Jena, long a centre of critical cultural and intellectual activity in the GDR, had already been one of the focal points of the protests against the expulsion of the singer Wolf Biermann in 1976. More recently attention has been drawn to the events surrounding and following the death on 12 April 1981, in the custody of the State Security police in nearby Gera, of the 23-year-old Matthias Domaschk. The official explanation that Domaschk had hanged himself with his shirt was met with scepticism by friends and acquaintances in his home town of Jena. Flowers were regularly placed on his grave—and equally regularly removed—and the anniversary of his death was marked by an obituary notice in the local paper and a rash of notices pinned to trees in the town.

The Domaschk affair rumbles on, and is becoming associated with other events and other names—like that of the young sculptor Michael Blumhagen, who was arrested (and later released to West Berlin) after placing a piece of sculpture— which was subsequently removed—in the cemetery in memory of his dead friend; or that of Roland Jahn, sentenced in January 1983 to 22 months in prison for riding through Jena on 1 September 1982 with a Polish pennant on his bicycle, bearing the words 'Solidarity with the Polish People'; or that of his friend the lorry driver and photographer Manfred Hildebrandt, who was sentenced in December to 16 months in connection with photographs he had taken of the incident, and pacifist postcards he had produced that were deemed a 'defamation of the State order'.

December 24 is for Germans a highpoint of the Christmas celebrations, and in 1982 a number of people in Jena decided to mark the occasion by gathering to observe a one-minute silence for peace outside a church in the town-centre. In the days leading up to Christmas Eve large numbers of those intending to participate in this 'Friedensminute' were interrogated by the State Security police, and warned to stay out of the town-centre on the 24th. From the early morning of Christmas Eve onwards, checkpoints were set up on roads leading into Jena as well as on the town station; young people from outside the town were turned away, and parents were warned to keep their children at home; the Working Class Combat Groups were placed on alert for a 'major action against the class enemy'. In the event some 200 people gathered nonetheless; some 40 of them—mainly parents with prams and young children—were sufficiently inconspicuous to get through the massive security net, and duly observed their one-minute silence. All were photographed many times over, and most were subsequently visited by security officials.

As a result of the Christmas Eve demonstration, at least a dozen further citizens of Jena were sent to jail. The authorities, in apparent response to an appeal from prominent representatives of the West German peace movement, denied that they were there because of their witness for peace. This was to be expected: demonstrating for peace is in itself not the offence that peace demonstrators—in East or West—are normally arrested for. More alarming from the point of view of peace activists in Jena was the public response of the Church: it simply disowned the demonstrators. In a letter to Western journalists, the press office of the—traditionally conservative—Thuringia district of the Evangelical-Lutheran Church wrote: 'On Christmas Eve, 24 December 1982, there were no activities of any sort outside churches and parish halls in the Jena area for which the Church can be held responsible' (*Frankfurter Allgemeine Zeitung*, 16 February 1982).

The negative response both of the Church and the State to the Christmas Eve events was in distinct contrast to their attitudes to the previous year's Dresden gathering. On 17 February the West German *Frankfurter Allgemeine Zeitung* published a letter to the Thuringian Church from 18 young Christians living in the Gera area expressing their 'shame' at the attitudes of their Church leadership, at its failure to support young Christian peace campaigners, over the death of Matthias Domaschk, and the disappearance of the Blumhagen sculpture. The Church still made no public response: indeed, it claimed that it had not received the letter, and there were expressions of doubt about its authenticity. And then, at the end of February, came news that all the Jena detainees had been released.

There is little doubt that discreet but firm pressure both from within the GDR itself—from the Churches and leading intellectuals—and from without—from foreign politicians and peace movement activists—played its part in the sudden easing of the increasingly tense situation in Jena. It would, however, be rash to draw any hard and fast conclusions from